RICH MIND

TO GET RICH, YOU HAVE TO THINK LIKE A RICH MAN.
HOW TO USE THE LAW OF ATTRACTION, A GUIDED
VISION TO ENERGIZE YOUR MIND AND
ACHIEVE YOUR GOALS

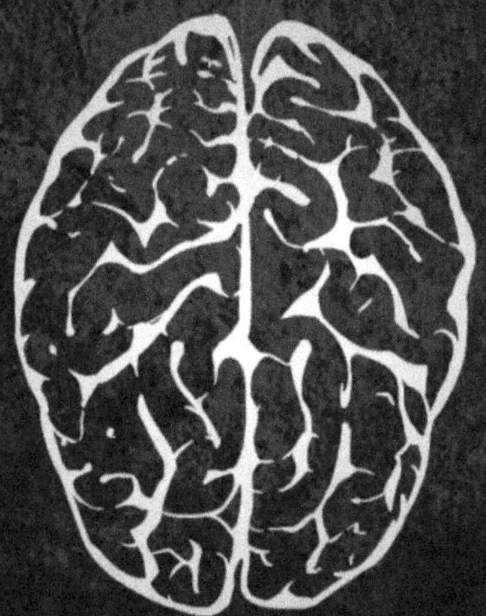

CHARLES EKERR

RICH MIND

To get rich, you have to think like a rich man.
How to use the law of attraction, a guided vision
to energize your mind and achieve goals.

VOL.1

CHARLES EKERR

Table of Contents

*Nothing happens in any aspect of
life, or business, without
something or someone moving.*

INTRODUCTION

The only disparity is the MINDS of the wealthy and the poor. Your emotional and mental will affect every part of your life, including your wellbeing, prosperity and happiness. A good mental outlook allows you to hit great financial altitudes. It is because you free your mind from negative emotions like fear, anxiety, rage, remorse, self-pity, revenge, hate, envy and greed by positive approach to your life.

Whenever you have these negative feelings, you waste a great deal of mental and emotional energy better geared towards achieving dignified and beneficial objectives. No space, regardless of how limited, in your mind should be allowed for negative thoughts and emotions. Your ideas, emotions, expressions, acts and responses must always be optimistic to fast progress along the road to wealth and achievement.

Your mind's optimistic attitude is enveloped by positive emotions like love, goodwill, harmony, joy, appreciation, success and positive anticipation. When a positive mental outlook is your way of life, you exude a true contagious optimism quickly and naturally, with a warm and friendly personality and a favorable experience. And when powerful people want your business, the doors are open to you.

When you live positively, you build the optimistic attitude
to life for which successful people are known: you think
positive, dress positive, speak positive, and act positive.
You're going high, chest out and face up. You function in
constant optimistic hopes and produce great results.

Rather of dwelling on suffering and poverty, fill your mind
with wealth and happiness feelings. Speak of
completeness and vitality instead of sickness and bad
health. Thinking of disappointment and loss, think of
accomplishment and achievement. Think chance instead
of impossibility.

CHAPTER ONE: CAPACITY IS A STATE OF MIND

This subject is very difficult to understand, easy yet hard to comprehend because it is so basic. This is why there will be several conversations about this in different ways so that you have the range of ideas that you can understand. Although there are several lessons on the same subject, they can be seen as part of a long lesson, in reality you can understand the idea from not just any single lesson but even a single lesson line.

Mind's essence is like rain. Since the air does not have a fixed shape, but takes the form of its jar, the mind also takes the form. It might be more easy to imagine of water right now, but once you understand the connection between mist and wind, let your mind get closer to air than mist.

In its liquid state, water is rather maltable. Yet put it in a jar and freeze it, break the jar apart and the water has taken this shape and stored it, instead of it being flowing.

The same goes for the real essence of the mind. This is still unformed, like before you were born and when you are still a infant. Yet as it blends in with an idea of what the world is meant to be, it takes a set shape. Then you are stuck with this shape and struggle to make the world fit.

Taking the water in a boat a step further frozen. Let's presume the vessel had in the middle a strong rod. Instead the water will emerge as a hollow core cylindrical. The mind is not only set in its shape, but still seeks to fit everything it finds into the shape of its hollow core. There are now two constraints on how life is treated. It needs life and the universe to be in a certain way, and instead needs everything and everything that it interacts with to match the definition of how it should be in its defined form.

Since a square pin doesn't fit into a round hole, truth doesn't fit in the frozen shape. And that's why truth is overlooked and life is difficult. Acceptance can not be accepted.

This solidification, rigidity, is never observed, since the mind feels free or at least like it is supposed to be. Having settled down in a shape such as cement, when it is almost liquid, but when it is hardened without ever being more liquid, and therefore believes it to be what it is for the rest of its life, it always takes that attitude. This is because we believe our body and personality to be what we truly are, rather than just a ship we are put in temporarily. Fortunately, the mind has the opportunity to go back to a liquid or even gaseous state. But it would allow the ice to be placed on the flames. As the Sufis say, you have to prepare.

There is a simple practice to melt the ice at all times. Remember that when you look at a remote entity, your mind is no longer separate from that thing, whatever it is, and that your mind is a flame of the same original fire, the essence of your soul, the god you are a flame and the entity you are contemplating. Enable your mind to get away from your body and expand like the air leaves a ball when the opening opens.

The real mind is the source of visual experience. It's not a thing, it's an aspect of a thing, the aspect of vision. That's why we compare it to air or to water as a contrast between fixed and maltable, 'a thing versus not a thing.'

As soon as you begin to feel connected, take the exercise one step further and try to understand the meaning of the interpretation of the image.

Let's go step by step; 1 See, let's say a mountain, a distant point.

2 Contemplate that the bodies and the mountains are all made of the same, atoms as well as the air within them. This could take some time, maybe ten minutes or more. Note that, in fact, you and the mountain, as well as everything between you and you, i.e. air, are the same,

atoms. When your hand touches something, your hand isn't your power, it's your brain's capacity, but the hand moves from the object to the brain. It's the same as the air between you and the mountain, it's the essence of the view, there's no difference.

3 If you feel a change in your perception or mental state, it's like opening a door or relaxing a tense muscle, (this can take several times of practice until you get it, so continue to do it as much as you can before you get it).

4 Try to see who looks at the mountain and the body and thinks about it. Or you might try to see how the mountain and your body are perceived.

5 Whether you know like you look or what you see, the source of interpretation in vision is the existence of your true mind.

On the second point, let's extend. When your hand touches something, it is not your touch, it is your brain's staff, so it binds the object to your brain. For example, if you touch a piece of fabric, maybe the finest silk, it will give you a feeling. And if you affect a person's skin, it will give you another feeling, particularly if the person is alive or only recently deceased, so that the body is still warm, or again whether they are of the same or opposite sex, whether they are relatives, or of slightly different ages. Moreover, if you hit the arm or nose, it will give the emotions different reactions again.

Explore your mind and understand how the surface of the object you touch is not the only explanation for how you perceive what you touch and how it affects you. Consider of the impact that the subconscious has on the physical senses. How different the mind is based on what you touch and what part of your body touches you, your hand or your face.

It is very interesting to see how the mind and emotions actually perceive our physical senses and thus regulate our experiences. If you've taken the time to let this sink in, you can begin to see how your programmed thoughts hinder your ability to grow in full.

You know (though you want to pretend that you do believe), that you can not move through walls or float in the air, or predict the future or read the minds of men. Yet the fact is that we can do these things, because other people can do it all. The structure of your mind, in its present solidified state, prevents you from doing such things.

The way to heat the mind and grow all of its potential is to kill its principles. This lesson helps you to test the validity of the senses. I have not only taught you to doubt your thoughts and convictions, but also to doubt your physical senses. This melts the ice of the defined mental shape. But before you can set the fire in the heat of a barren desert, where you will be faced with significant obstacles to change your shape, you must first prove through practices that all is in your head, and nothing you actually believe is as true as you believe it is. We erase the limits of our convictions. You will never allow the full potential of your being to emerge if you don't break them down first.

It's just the same as carrying big bags and burning your palms, but your fingers can't open when you put them down. Try it for three minutes. Close your fist as firmly as possible and just relax the hold for three minutes a day. Relax them, stop making attempts at the end of time, and you'll see how they maintained their position. Do not just open them aggressively and quickly, that will damage your hands, allow them to open naturally, and see how long it takes to relax completely.

For order to understand the lessons in this class, your mind needs to relax in the same way you have opened your hand again. You know how long the mind has been closed to its values, it will take time to open and the only way to do so is simply to let it relax, to stop worrying.

This is an easy way to relax your mind. When you are faced with someone who is upset with something and you disagree about it or does not seem right to you, note how your mind has clung tightly when it comes to defending your decision (you can also use it for something you are firmly committing like abortion as an example.

Note how the brain is tensioning. Then use the dissolving practice and let it melt, let it gradually relax as you did with your head. If you agree or disagree at the end of the discussion, who is right is not the issue. It's a chance to practice allowing your mind to melt and relax, free. This is another way you can grow your being at any point of the day without taking time out of your daily life to find ways to practice.

Subconscious and Conscious Mind

The subconscious mind is states of consciousness where knowledge of its use is employed in terms of personal growth and self-awareness as a means of achieving higher consciousness and mental awareness growth. The conscious and subconscious both reflect facets of mind and awareness linked to human consciousness that are connected to the way we experience life.

For example, the subconscious gives meaning in the language of symbols and pictures. The styles of concepts used in the subconscious are imaginative, innovative, convictions and abstract ways of thought. It also considers our early experiences and inherited behavior patterns related to our schooling and conditioning.

The subconscious holds the key to a higher understanding of thoughts and feelings, but their meaning and knowledge are useless when consciously and with consciousness articulated for some good purpose. The cycle of logic and raison, which makes them more concrete and better understood in their expression, filters subconscious meaning that passes to the conscious mind. Otherwise, what we do, say or refer to or about will not have any significance.

On the other hand, the conscious portion of the mind reflects our waking state and consciousness. Our sensory experiences provide outside world knowledge, which is then assimilated by our conscious thoughts and feelings. These are then sent to the under-conscious, where they are converted into convictions, wishes, or values, which in turn are interpreted by the conscious mind in the form of perceptions that perceive our lives as what they are and how we see them. All the knowledge about our life experiences is preserved as a memory in the subconscious.

The conscious mind itself often plays a role in the perception of other facets of the subconscious, such as the significance of words, linked to the perceptions and knowledge perceived outside of one's consciousness or if you prefer outside one's self-consciousness. Nevertheless, when understanding the higher level of consciousness, it is dependent on assistance from higher intellect networks of mental minds such as intuitive and soul- and spiritual dimensions of consciousness that come from deeper patterns of subconscious awareness in the higher states of mind.

If used in conjunction with self-awareness, the subconscious mind is three main components of the mind used to achieve higher levels of consciousness. We work together to characterize human and person consciousness as a whole's overall quality, existence and purpose. They discuss facets of the mind with regard to our human existence and perception of what life is and who and what we are and our relationship with being a part of the universal life force itself.

Higher consciousness It implies higher levels of consciousness as those which are appropriate for the intellect of the mind and the manifestations of the human soul and spiritual consciousness. In a larger sense, higher consciousness states of the person are linked to the consciousness of universal and spiritual entities that form the celestial streams of unconscious activities from which planes of the human stream of consciousness are just a part.

First of all, it is important to think that everything produced consists essentially of electromagnetic forces and particles of matter at varying levels of density. That includes also thoughts, feelings and any state of consciousness irrespective of which state it is. The mind of reason can be applied to and made meaningful when used properly and in conjunction with the subconscious mind consciousness and higher conscious states. If a person understands and understands something in his / her unconscious, it is possible to see not just how the subconscious patterns work but also how they function from a place of mental detachment where self-consciousness has been raised to a higher mode of expression of the consciousness that holds ample ground for the validity of that higher consciousness

When the goal in a developmental technique in higher consciousness requires a conscious understanding of the actions of subconscious forces, for the sake of clarification the mind calls upon higher energies of consciousness, for instance, those which are more refined and enhanced by the use of the power of will and intellect that originate from higher experiences of mind intellect.

The conscious decisions are made in these states about their life path, their soul intent and its meaning by the consciousness of a person and their higher expression of it and their subsequent subconscious expression. The ordinary waking consciousness of the daily consciousness of the mind may not recognize these subtle and essential choices. Because it is a higher self- and can not necessarily be recognized by the normal awakening conscious mind, they still exist as a form of higher guidance, posed in the aura of the person in the form of electromagnetic intellective consciousness states to which the higher mental consciousness states are more refined and cultivated.

Others might be completely unaware of these states, while others may be considered subconscious, while the higher consciousness states are aware of the subconscious whose rates are of a frequency and vibration intensity, while the range of senses is of a different nature and quality of consciousness, which is only perceived consciously, but only by t The difference is that they are actually called unconscious as they refer to what seems to be concealed from the conscious mind and physical world.

Moreover, conscious choices made in higher states of consciousness may not be fully understood or, indeed, understood later, only if a person wakens in a conscious state, unless they have a strong working knowledge of the operation of metaphysical laws and principles. Even when at that time self-confidence is not particularly based on subconscious behaviors related to higher consciousness conditions. Where this is always so, perception is confined to mental awareness as an unconscious part of the subconscious – or at least before the soul has built a bridge of awareness and they are ready to be accepted by it as the conscious cycle of development linked to their experiences in the field of physical emotions.

Conscious decisions made while in high-level consciousness are often for the good of the soul as they move through life to further enhance the conscious usage for their evolutionary purpose of the subconscious consciousness added to their physical, emotional and mental vehicles of consciousness.

For someone who takes the time to explore them inside himself, the benefits of higher consciousness are there. These are important tools for growth, which contribute to a broader understanding of life and to a great deal more deeply attached to its meaning and function.

There are different levels of human consciousness which all form the consciousness of the subconscious and the unconscious. Higher mental consciousness states such as universal-soul-spiritual-divine or celestial states; with the more general states of consciousness such as the physical-emotional-mental and intuitive existence, all of them are together in their varying degrees.

Both these states of consciousness are state or energy states in their most fundamental type in various densities in matter. The higher states are more refined mental consciousness energies whose dimensions are various modes of consciousness generated by the more subtle electromagnetic properties of matter. The type of consciousness is concealed as the capacity of mind in the nucleus of the soul's subatomic or rather subatomic (atomic means spirit) parts, before a given degree of self-awareness is developed enough to attract and emit the energies which are allayed to the emotional and mental modes of the soul and designs appropriate to its conscious apprehension.

Really unconscious are merely names that we offer to characterize our human actions with regard to our perception and thinking of higher understanding and mind consciousness, where we come to "learn," contrasted "which is understood" with that which still remains to be learned. The whole object of life, it seems, is to become more and more aware of it; to a greater degree of exposure to the powers of the conscious subconscious and unconscious, so that we can better understand life on the conscious level and see for what it is and, if possible, develop it with regard to our perceptions and thoughts and feelings as a result of our own.

It can not necessarily be achieved because the person's consciousness is perceived from a higher state of self-confidence that enables each level to be interpreted concurrently. This is induced by the intelligence of each person contributing to the state of greater consciousness; which we will call the soul for want of a better word if it pleases.

CHAPTER TWO: REMOVE NEGATIVE INFLUENCES

Growing individual has a unique aura that represents his current status. Those who are emotionally or ill have low, dark auras, while positive, healthy people have auras which are solid, bright auras. In blocking harmful forces from draining energy and vitality from us, solid, safe aura is important.

For an aura, there is no empirical description. Most scientists believe they don't exist. Others, although open-minded, can not scientifically explain auras. Many people view pictures as proof of auras, but others are doubtful about it. People with supernatural powers can still see and read auras. The halos you see can possibly be auras in traditional religious art.

Naturally, people with clear optimistic auras are charming and attract others. We seem to be more effective at getting things done and other people's help. Those who have negative auras are mostly self-promoters who scare others away and those who have powerful negative auras may be malicious. Negative auras may become parasite and literally steal positive auras from energy.

It is important to bear in mind that the aura has little control. The state of an individual is physical, psychological, emotional and spiritual. It is the instrument by which mental healers assess the overall health and well-being of a individual. A strong positive aura indicates that you have a solid, safe body, a good emotional and psychological wellbeing, spiritual maturity and power. A low or negative aura suggests physical sickness or disease, conflictual feelings, psychological problems unresolved and/or minimal spiritual growth. As you improve your aura, you move toward being a happier, more positive person with a stronger spiritual base.

Negative people can affect positive people and manipulate them. Psychics can actually see this in the interaction between auras, where the aura of the negative person appears to sap the aura of strength and light of the positive person. The optimistic person may sense it when he or she gets exhausted or weaker, loses his or her mood or may feel uncomfortable or anxious.

Positive people may also affect negative people, on the other hand. Your energy and vitality will flow into a person with a negative or weak aura literally. This is what supernatural healers do. Via their aura, they give the negative individual positive energy. So, the more the positive guy, the greater his aura, the less likely he is to steal his energy from a negative person.

Nobody wants to be around a person who is gloomy and constantly depressed. Since the negativity is contagious. It literally removes more positive people from the negative person. And, the stronger you are, the safer and happier you are, the more vulnerable you are to adverse effects.

What triggers poor auras?

People with negative auras, whether due to a physical, mental or spiritual disorder, frequently have severe illnesses. This will kill your aura to drink, smoke and narcotics. Heat, dispute and abuse can also happen. Too little exercise, mental stimulation, positive social interaction or spiritual relationship can lead to a weak dark aura. And unethical actions can be devastating-violence, misconduct, and your fellow man's misuse can create as dark and thick an atmosphere in the night. Negative auras can be incredibly strong, representing the internal chaos that causes them and can have a significant impact on the people around them.

Many people do not necessarily accept that harmful energy is correlated with a living human. The troubled minds of people who died before problems could be settled are an indication of a destructive force that could still affect the living. And as good spirits live, so are angels, so are evil spirits. Nothing can confirm or deny their presence, but many people have seen the strong effects of toxic bodies having an influence on their lives.

How do I guard against harmful energy and auras?

At the other hand, people with positive auras can better tolerate negative influences. Their good health is a high defensive barrier and their strength and vitality is less vulnerable to drainage. You have to be a better, more optimistic person if you want to have a better, more optimistic aura.

There are also strategies that we can use to shield against harmful energies and forces and preserve a balanced aura. All these methods are designed to make our psychic abilities more powerful and more receptive to external stimuli that could threaten us.

A significant first step is to learn to use your instincts and trust it. As starters, have you ever spoken to someone and had a knot shape in your stomach? This knot tells you that the individual is negative and can drain your strength. Relying on these inner signals may be one way to preserve your good energy and aura.

Many people, however, have difficulty separating intuitive and emotional awareness. Once you begin to improve your intuitive skills, you need to be careful not to let your emotions obscure an intuition. No school or college is there to explain the difference. The best way to learn is through testing and error, through self-confidence and ability to make mistakes.

It is important to look at your motivations. Maybe you've got the knot in your belly because you wanted to hit the person into the mouth. It's not intuition. It is feeling. Feeling. You are the only one capable of reading such signals, and self-knowledge is a vital instrument to discern intuition from irrational emotions.

Another way of being better, happier and happier is to stop losing or hurting items. Avoid junk food, caffeine, tobacco and drugs. They weaken your defenses and your personal determination. They cloud intuition and emotional development. Counterbalancing negative things means integrating good stuff into the everyday life-exercise, healthy foods, meaningful social interactions, prayers and meditation.

Meditation strengthens you and your aura. Hearing calming music or reading an inspiring or elevating book helps to clear up the mind and body of negative factors. Meditation helps you change externalities and adapt to your own strengths and experience. Meditation is a very necessary and satisfying method for a safer and more optimistic atmosphere.

You can also use other items that can heal or protect. Amulets are meant to kill harmful spirits. We come in several different forms, shapes and sizes and are made of various materials. Used by indigenous and tribal people since time immemorial, they can be worn as jewelry or carried in pockets or in bags. Many people use stones as amulets. Onyx, hematite, quartz double-terminated and aragonite are common stones for this reason. They are also known as defensive stones.

You can try to get a physical place to block it, if you believe you are being assaulted and someone or something is trying to drain your strength. The aim is to emotionally, physically and spiritually protect yourself at the same time. Take a stance that blocks external influences by crossing your arms and legs before your eyes. Tap the fingers on your right hand to render all the fingers on your left hand. Close your eyes, clear your mind and slow down until you feel relaxed and safe.

When you shut yourself off in this way, you won't just shield yourself from negative forces. This is a way to make a mental break and let your body and mind be refreshed and improved. In effect, your aura should be bigger, lighter and more immune to harmful influences.

Get Negativity Out of Your Life!

You claim that it is only through good stuff and positive people that you have a positive outlook and a happy life. What do you do then, when your relative, your best friend or even worse spouse has a negative impact on your life? If you actually want to take the constructive advice, you should dump them! We are both conscious that advice of this nature is simply not appropriate. So, what are you doing?

First, do you think that these people could be afraid unconsciously, if not consciously? Afraid you may grow beyond them and leave them behind? Fear that your success can decrease your own achievements or self-esteem? All these fears and more are very likely and have been stated here that you may take a different view. You turn pessimistic thinkers into a constructive way of thinking in the ideal world. Sadly, we don't live in a perfect world and we don't want to push others to think like you and me. Just this is what you do: take the positive step of embracing them – your mate, your wife.

We have the right to choose from others!

We are all entitled to choose. Nobody will drive us abroad. For those who are nearest to us, it is no different. We might not like their way of thinking or attitude. We may even think they are completely incorrect or out of control, but that doesn't change anything. All right, but let's say we do that. All right. How should we take that? We also get through these negative vibes. We've already decided that we can't change the individual, so the only one left is us.

When the negative shots are shot at us, what do we focus on? We were fired with the negative projectiles. Right? Right? If we agree that we can not change the individual, we must change our thought. This means how we think and concentrate on. The way we feel when we get negative details is nothing more than a reaction. Check your answer and win.

Standards.

When you have a new project, an idea, a personal enthusiasm you would like to share, you expect a particular reaction and would be very surprised if it does not occur. Note what happens when the strategy is reversed. I.e. I.e. If you don't have any expectations! Immediately, only the slightest positive gain is an enormous bonus! If you don't get it, it's no longer relevant, because you didn't expect it anyway! So, concentrate on the positive instead of concentrating on the bad.

Focus on the good! Emphasis on the good!

To a degree, you have to be one-minded, concentrating instead on your target at that moment. And, if you haven't done so already, get your goal firmly set. Determine how badly you really want it, and ask yourself whether you should pay the price or not.

Are you ready for payment?

Does that concern you? Payment of the price? It does not. Anything we do in this life needs a cost to pay. It's a financial number sometimes. Other times, it could just be time, etc. You still pay the price on various successes, big and small, every day. In this particular case the reason you pay the premium is such that negative feedback or factors actually do not have a leverage.

Trust completely in yourself, and you won't fail. As previously mentioned, many speakers of positive thinking lead you to be surrounded by positive people and a positive atmosphere so that you remain optimistic about everything you do. I have no doubt that if you can create such an atmosphere that it works! Picture the scene: in the morning you get out of bed, and the sun shines, the sky is blue. They welcome you with a kiss if you have a girlfriend. The smiling poster never holds charges. Everybody drives very happily and considerably on the way to work. Your employer is free to enter the air-conditioned building and you have the right amount of work to do to keep you motivated positively. It must be done -.snap your fingers! Wake up! Wake up! It can't just be done to this extent. Here I jest. I jest. I do believe that it will work for you to be surrounded by optimistic people, but it is unlikely that such an experience will last a very long time. This is the ideal world that we have described. The truth is, however, that we are not always living in this kind of world, and we surround ourselves with people who do not share our beliefs, our ideals or our enthusiasm. Too what? It could be our friends, our relatives, or worse, our wife. Should we go away and curl up somewhere in a corner and forget whatever "crazy idea" we had? No. No. Of course not. Of course not. What would otherwise be the point of being involved in some good idea! No, the trick is to understand the people you involve mentally and evaluate those who help, think and be constructive.

Get a good shot!

These will be the kind of people who don't blindly say "go for it, well done," but who really inspire you to grow, step forward, and make yourself something. Now, take a minute û. Let your book of addresses out. Go through it and then show someone you know can count on for you. Those friends and family who matter about you and trust you and trust your successes and can give you the support you need. What you don't need is compassion. What you need is a supportive infusion of those you can count on when you're targeted. When times are complicated, that's your reserve. Let me say how you can plan another reserve. And you can manage at a moment's notice. One that when you dive into it gives you almost a moment the optimistic impulse.

Your Positive Booster for Power!

Take your hardback notebook and pen and start writing. Don't write about something old, but concentrate on your achievements. Write about your achievements. Write it down and the pages float with passion and excitement as you talk of what you've accomplished and achieved. It could be big projects or minor activities that were significant items you achieved. Keep running. Keep moving. If you feel up to it, fill the journal. Connect to the book as much as you can and remember more accomplishments. If you do not write on the paper, make sure that it is readily available and does not leave it on the shelf to accumulate stain. During those times where disappointment is impressed, take the opportunity to open up and unwind in the pages of your success story. Know yourself. Know yourself. Relive those moments right there and see yourself. Remember the emotional elation you felt then. It is your positive energy booster that will drive you beyond the negative rise and place you on the way to your goals. Need more yet? Let's think about what you believe. What you believe.

CHAPTER THREE: PARADIGMS OF INTERDEPENDENCE

It is not unprecedented for anyone in today's world to identify oneself as 'independent.' You might do this as though you speak about something that is a common part of life or do it with a sense of pride.

And In the first instance, you may have lived life like this for quite a long time, and you don't have to know that you do something special. With this, they are likely to be able to support themselves financially.

Yet even though they haven't lived life in this way for a long time, they still don't have to do anything. This may be a indication that they know what the other side is like, and so they should be incredibly thankful.

Proud If you're just too happy to think about how "alone" you can be a sign you haven't been this way for a long time. Yet even though they do, they still feel the need to let other people know how they live.

Therefore, it is not enough for them to support themselves financially, for example, they would have to take it further. And though they may be thankful, they are likely to concentrate more on how well they have performed.

Dependency Such people may claim that they were "dependent" before they were "independent." In being this way, they could claim that they do not financially support themselves.

The money they got from other people should have come and that means they should have been paid. The money they have today is the product of hard efforts, and it reflects that they have worked for it.

In fact, they might claim that they should take care of their own emotional needs. Through doing so, you can suggest that you need nobody in your life and that you can do it by yourself.

This view may mean that they avoid romantic relationships and not just that; they also might not have close friends. And while they could have families around them, they could do whatever they could to keep them at some distance.

However, if they end up in a relationship with someone, they are unlikely to have an intimacy, because they will probably not be able to let go. Through having to do it alone and remain "strong," it might keep them from becoming insecure and from communicating really with another person.

This could also mean that they may have 'casual meetings,' because they will not need to be vulnerable in such interactions. And while they may have mates with the same perspective, they also come in touch with others in need.

When you are in this role and can support yourself financially, it is obvious that you are not financially dependent on others. However, even if they play an important role in what happens, it does not mean they are not dependent on anybody.

First of all, at the end of every month, they will rely on their employer to pay them. Also, if you are self-employed, you must rely on the money of your customers.

So before you even come to work, you will rely on your car or train to get there, and if you walk there, you will rely on the roads or paths that other people have created. If you are self-employed and you operate from home, you must rely on a computer designed by other people and an Internet connection managed by others.

But to get even that far they'll have to eat and drink, and even if they can grow their food they will still rely on the earth. There's also the air you need to survive.

Interdependence What this shows is that one could say that they are interdependent. And while they may like to believe that they don't need anyone, this isn't a fact.

Many people play a crucial role in their ability to survive on and without help on this planet; their lives will be very different. This doesn't mean that you need one person in particular to survive; it means that you need others in general.

Terrible Twos

When a child turns 2nd, he or she will possibly have to break away from his or her caregiver to experience life alone. During this time, the child must go and return, and this will take place for a while.

The child will assume during this time that nobody else is needed, but he will quickly start to be worried if his caregiver is not there when he returns. Therefore, even though the child may behave independently, it is nothing more than an illusion.

A Reaction At this age, the ability of the child to think will not be fully developed so it should view life differently. When it comes to an adult, though, they won't be in the same place and that means they are able to see how interdependent they really are.

Even, if you have not fulfilled your needs during your younger years, you might make them go to the other extreme and behave as if they were unnecessary. During these years they should have felt embarrassed that they had needs and that they should behave as though they didn't have to feel this pain.

Toxic Pain

However, the suffering they feel would not be as unbearable as the pain they would be if they had contact with how they felt all those years ago. We are undoubtedly toxic, and by disconnecting themselves from this guilt, we will be confused and then it would be natural for them to lose contact with their humanity.

One consequence is that they behave as though they're more normal, and that means they feel that they don't need others. Depending on what happens as a infant, needs are seen as shortcomings and so it is important that they cover their needs.

Conscience

When you're in this place and you find it difficult to acknowledge that you need help, it's crucial that you express the pain inside you. If this occurs, they will agree that they are interdependent.

Developing Healthy Boundaries

What are limits? The laws governing relationships are boundaries. Every partnership has laws and, even though we are not always aware of them, we generally know intuitively what they are. Borders that fall into three categories and can be described as follows: rigid borders are inflexible borders. Check out "Ordinary People" for a snapshot of what this sort of boundary looks like. In this film, the family, affected by the death of the youngest son, has formed rules to deal with his grief, rules that include not crying, not thinking about the son or his death and, last but not least, not feeling something. The healing of the family starts when these laws break down. The remaining son points out that it is not possible to live up to these laws, and eventually discovers that family members are more insecure, even when violating the rules. Strong family boundaries keep feelings closed and unchanged. The long-term costs of this form of boundary may be the inevitable family breakup. However, if there is no total disintegration, family members eventually lack closeness as each person is involved in his or her own activities. And when there is a problem, the family can not work together.

The second form of limit is called an embedded limit. The family functions and communicates in a very closed environment. The closed family system means that the family is very close to each other-to the full. The family is so close that people in the family unit have no privacy. It can be really hard for everyone to believe that everybody knows every aspect of their own business. This can happen, for example, if an individual of the relationship suffers from addiction and the goal of the family is to help that person. This can also contribute to a similar co-dependency type. With this trend, family members have no privacy and it is not rare for someone without permission to access another person's private room. It is very difficult for individuals to build clear sense of themselves within this form of family environment, when all their efforts are focused towards the advancement of family goals.

Where people are interdependent, the best kind of borders create. People are very supportive of each other in a family with interdependent ties but each person has a sense of personal control over his or her actions. A family is strengthened instead of threatened when each person has his own activities.

Generally, people with interdependent relationships have better ties. This is because people are secure in understanding that they can go and do what they can do with their families, but they are free to enjoy one another when they return to the family relationship. Persons in interdependent relationships are free to discuss and ask their partner for their thoughts on topics because they know they'll love and support the other person in the relationship no matter what. However, if people disagree on an topic in a relationship, the other person will value the decisions the individual makes and will support each other.

Looking at the details and seeing the working advantages of interdependent connections, you may think that' it would be great if my relationships were real. 'The good news is that it is possible to change the boundaries of your relationships at present, but work is required. All relationships have their own rhythm and flow, so that changing patterns requires time and effort. Changing untouched boundaries can also be a painful and challenging process and can not always work if the individual is reluctant to adapt in relation to you. When necessary, discuss this with the other person before you agree to alter the boundaries in a relationship. When the other person is not open to improvement, you may have to decide the boundaries you need to define in the relationship.

Laws in relationships Everyone in a family knows the laws control relationships. You won't see the list of rules when you step into a family room, but everyone who lives there knows what they are. You know the rules only from living in your home.

Stand for a minute, what are your family's rules? Is that, don't cry, don't believe, or don't feel it? When you don't ask, try to crack the alleged law to see what's happening (just one word of caution ... don't do so during a holiday or a family celebration!). Notice the reaction, and what people do to try to make you turn into the desired actions when you violate the law.

I want to answer what I meant by "turn back" in the last paragraph before we move on. When we have relationships with others and try to change something that we feel needs to be changed, the other person may act so as to encourage them to return to their former behavioral pattern. It can make it so difficult to change the rules. If you are very committed to help improve the relationship, expect others to fight you every step of the way most definitely, because people don't like improve. Also, if possible, chat freely about the laws you want to change with the other person. It can help alleviate frustration in the person who does not know why you do not respond as he or she is used to.

The process of transition always occurs as people want to alter behaviors. If someone wants to alter their approach to events, the second person may behave in a manner that allows the first person to return to his or her usual behavior. It can be a very painful process if a person is committed to improving his or her behavior. However, the new action is finally recognized with consistency. Often, if possible, the best way to deal with the situation is to speak freely with the other person.

Now that we've decided which limits are, consider the measures you should take to reach safe limits.

Evaluation of the need for limits

1. Identify relationships in your life: relations with your spouse, relatives, colleagues, friends, etc.

2. How do you feel about your friendship with these people? In other words, do you want to spend time with the kid, or do you secretly hate taking time

3. Are you free to share your feelings with these people or do you find you can not openly share your thoughts with them?

4. Does the individual in your relationship value your views on issues? Or is he or she trying to change your mind?

5. Does the person you think about helping you or trying to speak to you about doing something else?

6. Is the person respecting your privacy or tending to take care of your personal affairs?

7 Do you want your relationship to be different with this person?

If you replied yes to all of these questions, you may want to create those boundaries.

Development of healthy borders

1. The first path to safe boundaries is to determine what changes you want to make in your relationship. For instance, in your life you may have someone who calls you too late in the night. After he or she fails to call you warn the person earlier that you will not be able to respond to the telephone after some time. After the limit is set, be careful and do not respond if this person still calls you late. Recall the next day and, if he or she protests, remind the person of the boundary gently but firmly. It may be challenging depending on the relationship, but with patience, things can improve gradually.

2. Make improvements to your own actions to enforce the boundary.

3. When you just want to make the change, and though the other person gets angry, hold the change.

4. Speak frankly and freely why you want this relationship to be improved. Tell the other person how they feel.

5. The other person should respect you and consider improvement in a healthy relationship.

What to do if the other person does not embrace change

1. Speak about how the other person thinks about the transition and what he or she will like to consider.

2. Discuss why things can't go back to their own way

3. Negotiate an agreement with the person with whom you will stay.

4. When you still can't fix the problem, you should determine if you can continue the way things are, and if not, determine what to do. Please consult a counselor to consider your options.

CHAPTER FOUR: UNDERSTANDING POSITIVE THINKING

Do you really wanted something to enrich your life forever? Do you ever notice something was lacking, but you didn't know what? Have you set and fallen short of targets? For many of us, you undoubtedly fall into a dark slump and gave up hope of a better future. The topic of self-amelioration is massive, and many lessons have to be taught. However, these are the first steps that provide the most insight and change our lives the most. Therefore, it is important to start with a technique that provides you with the best foundation on which to work and is very easy to learn. If anyone offered you a program of this kind, will you obey it or give it up?

The influence of positive thinking is well recognized, but still ignored. Apparently depressed people view the universe in a far more rational way. An optimist has no rational point of view. Where pessimistic loose are at their gloomy point of view of "today" and extending it into the future. A depression produces an uncompromising outlook on the future-one in which they make rational demands and predict great deceit. Like a prophecy that fulfills itself, they are typically correct.

The optimist uses constructive thought methods and sees the opportunity of everything. It provides a plausible future that motivates and pushes him forward. He gives himself straightforward, motivating priorities and wishes that inspire his acts. He has the problems of what the depressed call "unrealistic expectations." This challenge stimulates progress to further inspire the optimist towards his goals, a major factor in real happiness. When he is beaten, he knows that "try again but be more imaginative." The optimist constructs his own vision, inspired by his imagination.

As we can see, the influence of positive thought is a precious weapon that can be used to transform lives and make dreams come true. However, there are shockingly few clear sources of concrete knowledge, down to earth, about how to practice positive thinking. I am sure that you do not want to be stripped of the benefits it can offer, and undoubtedly you have found ambiguous and imprecise constructive directions that you have easily abandoned. If you believe like you can stick to four basic principles for at least a year, you will be amazed at the improvements like simple technology can bring. I am now introducing to you the four fundamental principles of positive thinking:

1) You are not your guy.

You're not your personality. You probably were different from what you are today as a kid. There is definitely a grain of resemblance, however much of what you do day after day, even if you might name it. It's not your personality. Rather, the so-called personality is a set of behaviors created by interactions as a protection to manage daily life. You should keep your imaginary personality back in life as it determines what you can do and what you are unable or unable to do. A woman can feel she can't talk effectively because she was shy all her life. It obviously doesn't happen; she actually needs to learn what makes a successful public speaker and follow such mannerisms herself.

For order to be truly successful for positive thinking, you must understand that you are not a set definition, no matter what age you are. You may be what you want to be. Often, we want to do things in which we feel confident. We say we will never go skydiving or anything like this. These opposing wishes are so significant. You will take them and make them come true. You're the way you want to open yourself to new experiences, to break out of the jail you call personality.

Choose one thing you never did but were always curious about today. Create a list of months of things you will not be able to do. Run a marathon, join the local drama club, spend a whole day outside without the office check-in. You are shocked how motivated you feel – and this gives you extra incentive to change your so-called identity.

2) Learn how to get inspired.

Most of us believe we're at the mercy of the day. We will do well on a well day, and on a bad day we will not be inspired, dodge, and do nothing. You must embrace the fact that your day is yours and you are only capable of reacting to the circumstances. Forward planning may provide protection by contingency plans to deal with what is perceived as unexpected. For those issues that tend to occur, see if there is a permanent way to solve them. When you have the situation as much as possible, the next growing field of motivation must be established.

For many of us, particularly the new ones to better ourselves, our emotions dominate our day. Or our lack of capacity to direct our own feelings. Motivation occurs because we are conscious that we have a mission that challenges us, is not insurmountable and provides a valuable outcome. In ensuring that all your main duties are in these sections, you can help to unleash your everyday activities.

Secondly, plan the office so that disruptions can be that. Have ready water source, fresh pencils and paper nearby. Make sure the distractions are as few as possible. Before that, you should concentrate on ways to boost your own mood – through have a playlist of your favorite songs. Create a list of the prioritized activities of your day and check them as you go forward. Getting a written record of your successes is an excellent way of building trust to complete tasks.

You can feel much more in charge of your workplace until you can organize and use the power of certain tasks for yourself. This additional protection will help you to develop self-confidence and to see things more positively.

Create a list of activities today and see if you can inspire.

3) Be confident about who you are.

Often people will bring you down consciously or unknowingly. You may be aware of your pronunciation, your weight or your lack of confidence. At the time of the attack, intense pain and ruin can sting and ruin your day or even longer. They lower your view of your own worth and trigger a negative spiral which sabotages any positive thinking. I encourage you not to be a victim and concentrate on something important, rather than to focus on why the other person did what they did. Having a victim will never yield a good result. This embodies feelings of helplessness and is subject to other people's whims. If there is some way you can stop feelings of victim status and use criticism positively.

You probably think-this is simple to say-but what is important is that you label 'insert insult.' I believe you should use criticism like fuel to show the other person's error-to realize that who you're today doesn't have to be who you are tomorrow, or next week, or next year.

If you are unhappy with what you have criticized, then choose if the time is right now to do something about it, and to overshadow the critical critic with his own strength. People who criticize also tend to believe that any question they perceive or "want to perceive" will still afflict you. It reveals to you and to the world that you can become anything you want to be if you can change it. Do not allow yourself or others to describe you as a stagnant being that will still be burdened by the same afflictions.

4) Create the future-commit yourself.

Imagine it's now a month. You have worked on the above three concepts and see progress. So that you learn to deal with your own issues, you can inspire yourself to a degree and shift your own borders – the time to build your own future. A life so far away from where you were a month ago, or even now, it would have been impossible to imagine before. You may want to be a model, lose weight, or increasing your income significantly. Maybe you want to go on stage or start a performing career in some popular theater. Look in the future for 20 years and decide where you want to be, irrespective of viability or shame. So, address this dream in clear words, like I'm going to weigh 20 pounds less or drive an Aston Martin.

Now take these details and imagine a scene that highlights all these points in your mind. Picture your future self on stage, beautiful and smiling. Now make the image wider and the colors clearer, smile and touch thumb and finger. Do this technique of visualization every day as many times as you recall. Often press thumb and finger together as you smile and picture the image coming to life. By so doing, we tie the vision for the future to a tangible practice. When you feel nervous or unmotivated from this point forward, press your thumb and forefinger together and you will receive a boost of strength and joy.

The Myths About Positive Thinking

A positive attitude adds to our lives for happier years and is recognized as the formula for success. It will help us to make a profit for a product. Families have proven that they help children who are happier and wiser. Smiling makes us physically more attractive and generally better. Therefore, nobody wants a party pooper to hang out. So, what went so wrong with the positive thinking theory that we had trouble applying it? Here are some ideas that you may have come to know about ....

Myth 1: Mystical is positive thought. Simply believe and satisfy your wishes. Dream of positive thoughts and all will happen instantly and you will relax automatically.

This is so incredible that these stuffs are hard to believe. No one has yet, to my knowledge, found the Genie lamp. It's not positive thinking that can't change your life and make you feel magical. In my life this worked miracles and fulfilled my dreams. And there was no magic involved. The thought and confidence that my dreams come true all led me to the hard work, creativity and determination to achieve them. The thought did not achieve the final result. The idea got me to the point that I could make the changes and actions needed to produce the final results.

Myth 2: You can deactivate it only. Think hopeful and watch your dream life grow from now on. Forget the bad emotions absolutely.

Are you reading enough books to believe this could happen? Have you ever said, "I'm going to be more hopeful from now on?" You can't shut your mind off or try not to think. It is a workout: don't think of a pink elephant. Imagine, not a pink elephant, what you want.

Okay, what do you think?

The term "positive thought" is tricky. Perhaps it's a more sophisticated way of saying Positive Filter. Change the means in which these ideas enter the mind instead of attempting to understand it. We can be surrounded by negativity, but we can opt out. We are surrounded by too much positiveness and should focus on it. That's what you want to concentrate on, which makes it good or bad. The goal is to make it realistic so that your mind takes it rather than just a casual exercise.

First of all, do you rather speak of his triumphs than about someone else's shortcomings? So, you should rely on great people who do amazing things if there is none? Can you talk about your hopes, dreams and happy life changes or a recent or funny meeting instead of listing all your misfortunes and talking with a friend? Would you like to focus on openings in your life, rather than dwelling on not having a job? And think about the value of things you have in your life (family, friends, health, skills, whatever). It gives you the state of mind required in any situation to have peace.

Myth 3: Better experience is a more positive human.

Usually, negative is deep-seated habits, and like many of these behaviors it is difficult to break. This is the cause for many of our other harmful behaviors. Are you being able to get used to it? How hard is it to give up a bad habit? It is known and accepted as all our basic habits, so it is fast. And, what if you were advised that your activities are harmful to both your physical and mental well-being? Will you change it? Will you change it?

It is difficult to move from negative to positive because many of our negative elements are related to our own self-image. How we think is true of ourselves and those around us, what we were taught, what we all learn and understand when we were young. It's not natural to let go of what we know to be true. We can also feel dumb and crazy at first. We will be these oddballs! We shall be these oddballs! Downright ridiculous!

In reality, some of us have a negative link with our loved ones. This is what we are talking about, what we feel together, and it is troubling that leaving misery will cost us so much. Negative thought is a breeding ground for many of our other unhealthy behaviors, which we can't ignore: overflood, drinking, avoidance, serious addictions, illness etc. So, what will a challenge be done? Take incremental steps to get going and do not expect sudden progress.

Here are a couple of things you can do at once. To begin with, to realize that positive thought can be as contagious as negative. You may be the leader in your party to change the subject or to make a light observation of the dark stuff. You may also decide whether other people may be too risky and it could be time to limit their length or strength. Or you can need to handle these relationships more closely and set these limits.

The argument is that you may have to give up some of the things you want to be. This calls for the reassessment of relationships. This is not always easy and can be a daunting challenge, but it is worth it if you are ready to rebuild your life.

Myth 4: A healthy mentality means that everything is all right, no matter what.

In the universe, life happens; some aren't very pretty. There are disasters for the world, global instability, wars, illnesses, malnutrition, economic problems ... How can such a planet find tranquility and positivity? When you do not profit from a situation, focus on the solution and act. It instantly improves your mental health! When there is no response and your views show no positive outcomes, you will need to evaluate your options and why you want to concentrate on them.

Practicing positive thinking involves forecasting pleasure, satisfaction, health and the progress of all situations and acts. This means that we hope for positive outcomes while we can prepare and be at ease with the unexpected, unintentional or apparently unsatisfactory. In less than optimum conditions, it is normal and safe to prepare. It is necessary to learn to face any circumstance or obstacle. Consider any trip as fun rather than stressing and focusing on numbers. When we follow the brighter path, positive outcomes are more likely.

Turning a blind eye to reality is not a sign of positive thought and caution against the tempest! The denial is a sign of depression. A pessimist may not want negative results or neglect issues. A critical thinker looks at all – obstructions, possible end results, inconveniences ... – find ways and means of coping with it in a given situation or at least trust yourself to deal with it effectively.

It will take time to develop a positive mind state to achieve a positive mind state, but I found it both entertaining and significant. Many of the instruments I use are everyday statements, creative images, encouraging speech, expressing gratitude, a vision screen and meditation. Both these techniques must be adequately educated and used to succeed.

Positive, happy people, inspirational books, uplifting films and avoiding negative media are easy and practical ways to begin thinking positively right now. Self-hypnosis and meditation are another useful method for your own use.

These goods allow you to pursue your lifestyle and better your life if you need it.

So also feel free to stick to the old message: "If you can't say anything positive, don't say anything." Don't be liable in the event of destructive thought that starts or continues as wild and dangerous flames. Note that it is a decision, that is, and it is up to you, to make the change a more confident person and to take these positive thinking behaviors.

CHAPTER FIVE: DEFINING WHAT YOU WANT IN YOUR LIFE

The Power of Transparency represents the final step of life change and real achievement. Another way to put it is, "What you see is what you get." You and you alone are responsible for the results that what you do or do not accomplish in your life, and no one else is responsible for it. You have complete power of your own destiny. Success, not chance, is a matter of preference.

The Inner Game-Your Attitude is about holding the keys to your own achievement. Before you say "shift inwards and shift the outside," you misunderstood me. What we're saying here is that your understanding and belief system about who you are or not is your fact, your facts. It is very small until you transform who you are in your ability to alter and understand those outcomes.

Responsibility means taking responsibility for your life as it is now and who you are. You understand and agree that you produce all that has occurred, good or bad, in your life. You can't change and you won't evolve until you stop looking outside and stop blaming others or keeping them accountable for certain circumstances in your life. If you are responsible for everything in your life, then you will take control and change your life.

One of my favorite phrases with respect to responsibility is, "The buck stops here." When I am coaching anyone and they make a particular person accountable for their decision or apologize because they haven't reached a goal, I would ask them this question, "Is someone holding a gun to their head?" You can feel like you have been forced or coerced, so you don't feel responsible, to do something you don't want to do. You and you alone have made the decisions you have made. Many of us forget in moments of tension that we have the free will to decide what we really believe in and what is in our best interest.

If, in your lifetime, you have an important decision to make, pause and consider before making the decision, it's not a case of life and death, take your time to consider about the options you have. Say to myself, does it advance my purpose to fulfill my dream or vision, or will it drive me away from my own dream and vision, if I make that decision? When you use this basic check and balance program, I can assure you that you are less affected and more goals accomplished.

You have found that many family members and friends are professionals for what you want in your life; the goals you want to accomplish are the dreams you want to realize. Most times the explanation is tragic enough that they have no aspirations or dreams, so that they connect with people who do. Have you also found that what these people have to say or share about your aspirations and dreams is not often very helpful? No, they usually dissuade you from big dreams because they don't have anything, or if they do, they don't have what you need to follow through with it and make it a reality in their lives. Thanks to the lack of concentration, ambition and trust in their life, they can't really be a happy leader for you and your life. It doesn't make sense!

There is nothing you can, do or have until you do achieve the desired alignment, only your own life experience can validate both your alignment only your intentions. Aligning with your inner self You have to take the time to know who you are and what you want to be. You'll live other people's fantasies if you don't know who you are; you're never going to have it if you don't know what you want. It is important to realize that if you want to improve your life, it is up to you entirely.

Personally, my life didn't really change until I was more and more responsible for my decisions and my future. You ought to reconcile yourself with who you are and who you will be. When you figure out what you don't want in your life, you realize what you want. However, you need to recognize the distinction; it is your attention to what you don't want which creates unwanted experiences in your life. In other words, you know what you don't want, but once you know what that is, don't concentrate your mind on this thought or feeling, concentrate on what you want to manifest in your life.

Great results start with great dreams, but a dream without a plan is just a vision. You need to have a vision of what you want to do and be responsible for the results. Dreamers dream big dreams, but they get results. Your dreams are yours and yours alone, so why then would you keep others in possession of your dreams? You can have something you dream of, but you have to do it and take action.

What people's mind can understand and believe can accomplish. You know that nothing will happen until it does. Achievements are what I call "pick-on-able," which you can pick on to obtain the desired outcome or outcome.

Inspiration I am referring to the degree of emotion and commitment, not by pure encouragement, but by much more strong emotion ...... inspiration. Inspiration is directly related to your aim and vision. It comes from the Latin word for inspiration, that is, to breathe on and on you. Inspiration is an internal feeling, whereas external motivation. It's much easier to be accountable for your day, ambitions and dreams if you're motivated, very excited about them.

Unless you are just driven, you will be knocked down by the first bump on the slope, and you can never climb back up. If you're motivated, sleeping powers you never knew could emerge from inside you. You become more aware of your sense of self and of the infinite capacity and possibilities of your being. Your imaginative degree comes to life and fresh ideas can spill like sweets at your corner shop from your subconscious. You will feel a sense of independence and a kid like curiosity you've been experiencing since your childhood and will feel young again.

Tag You're It People who are not responsible for their own lives are vulnerable to following the wishes of others. If you do not pursue your intent, your passion, your dream, you will follow someone else for a moment. By this point it's important for you to realize that you're not a passenger on the 'life bus.' You're driving, you must take over, chart the tracks, and then steer the bus in the direction you want them to go. It's your ride, there's nobody else. It's your life, so why would someone else take over? Don't allow someone to drive your cab, get into your drivers 'seat and drive your "life cab."

Facts to Achieve Great Success in Your Life

Everyone wants their lives to be good, they want great success. But only a few percent of them really accomplish what they want in their lives. Why is that? There must be something else and something successful people do that separated them from the others that would never achieve what they want in their lives.

And what have effective people done? Why do they vary from average people and why in their lives should they do what they want? I bet you know the answer, there's no trick, but it's because of these people's attitude and behaviors. Every successful person knows that they must follow the behaviors and habits of successful people in order to accomplish what they want in their lives, they must behave as successful people, be drinking and breathing and eat like them.

You can achieve the same results only by observing what effective people do. Below are the top 5 user-friendly facts, if you are to succeed a lot in your life.

1. Get Eliminate Your Comfort Zone That is the truth you will accept; success is not an easy job, and without hard work you will not have success. In other words, in this universe there is no free lunch. If you want it, you're going

to have to pay for it. The same goes for you, if you want to excel a lot in your life, you must be able to give your time and to make an effort. And this can only be achieved by pulling yourself out of your comfort zone.

You will never take the required measures if you remain in your comfort zone, which will bring you great success. Many people just think about performance and dream about it. You say you want to produce great results in your life, but you end up watching TV instead of acting to make your dreams come true. You have to get out of your comfort zone right now, if you are one of them. If you live in your comfort zone, you will never change and you will never achieve something. As the words say, you prefer to avoid change when you're too relaxed and never do anything to stretch you out to your potential.

2. Be 100% Dedicated This is another truth of the old generation. You know you will dedicate yourself to great success. If you're not committed, think you're going to do something you want to do? When you ask people to succeed in their lives, they are going to give a simple yes. But, when you ask them if they are 100% dedicated to success in their lives, they can pause for a moment and think about the answer. It indicates that they don't make 100% commitment, because in fact they realize that if they make a 100% commitment, they will achieve it.

Most people do not, however, make a 100% pledge. And this is why most of them do not excel in their lives. And if you read this right now, make sure you bring 100 percent of it into your life to accomplish what you want. When you don't make a 100% effort, you will possibly struggle and waste all the time and energy you put in. So, if you wanted to do something, why don't you do it best?

3. You need to have the burning desire That is the burning desire for great success which most people lack. Have you noticed the disparity between successful people such as Donald Trump, Warren Buffett, Michael Jordan, Steve Jobs and the ordinary? -- successful individual has this key to success, that is to say, they want to succeed. A burning desire is not like a mere wish or hope. A burning desire is everything you need. Without it, you can't exist. You must always do whatever it takes to do it.

And this is the secret you need to achieve the great success you want. Whenever you have the ability to burn, you're going to behave from another hand. You have set your goals as a must and you will do whatever you can to achieve them. Therefore, you must face each challenge and take drastic action to make it happen. So today, find out why you want to achieve great success in your life and grow your burning wish.

4. Every successful person sets their goals Well, not every successful person sets their targets, but 90%. So, as I told you above, follow the footsteps of successful people if you want to succeed. Do what they do, and just like them, you will produce the same amazing results. If you set your targets, you will also set your goals. I think you know about the target and why it is important to you.

With targets, you know where you will go and where your destination is. You will never be centered in your life if you don't have a target today. And if you don't focus on your career, you're everything you want to do, but you're never going to make real efforts. In the end, you will accomplish nothing. However, if you set your target and focus on it, the story will be different. You put all your strength in your target, just like a laser beam to smash something into it. Remember to set your goals, without goals great success won't come.

5. Nothing will happen without action Yes, if you have read this book but have not taken any steps to make your dreams real, nothing ever will happen. Nothing will happen. When awareness and skills are the catalyst for your performance, action is the driving force behind the catalyst. Do not ever expect success, it's not about waking up one day, and you are the CEO of a really successful business. It's not like you wake up one day and your bank account contains $1 million.

They won't all occur automatically. You really need to take some initiative, only then can stuff happen. Even if you have a magic button to succeed, you will need to move your hand to the mouse and hover it to press. Not all is going to happen automatically in this universe. Let things happen instead of waiting for things to happen.

It all happens, for a reason. Find the justification and do stuff. Start taking small measures to get you every day to your great success. Success is a process, not a destiny. It's all about applying your feelings. As soon as you read to this point, it shows only that you passed the first God exam. Take great achievement as your life's greatest challenge.

Visualization is the ability to see visual representations which are not present in our physical or real world. Such pictures of the mind are brought on by expressions, ideas and inductions. Normally a clinician or a skilled hypnotherapist uses imagination for a certain mood or state of mind.

Clinicians, relaxation practitioners, hypnotherapists and doctors used metaphor extensively. For instance, a doctor often gives a patient a visualization exercise before and after surgery. This visualization would aid the patient in the process of healing.

Throughout real life, many people successfully use visualization to change their lives and to gain wealth and prosperity. The power of imagination can also be used to get what you want in your life. Concentrate on your mental image or concept regularly. Many people have found that the development of images in their minds and emotions helps them accomplish more effectively what they want in life.

Some people believe they can envision clearly or see images in their eyes while others say they can't envision at all. Some people would say, when they are targeted at visualizing or attempting to do it themselves, nothing happens in their minds. The word vision does not mean that we use our actual eyes, but that we only recall visual images. And when appropriate we can picture or envision things in our minds and the information will be taken care of by our subconsciousness.

As people relax and allow their bodies to be part of the imagination process, they are able to appreciate the mental pictures as if they were at the present time. The only prerequisite for events to happen quicker is for you to visualize mentally, as they happen now. The other trick is to believe that everything you see now happens.

How is visualization so important to demonstrate?

By concentrating on the thing that you want to manifest, you motivate it to grow and evolve. We are both resources and interconnected. The thinking is energy and flies easily. Yet if you do not adequately feed them with images or sentences, random thoughts do not carry you to where you want to go.

Pictures and thoughts have their own magnetic energy which attracts similar energy. If, for example, you want to offer a better work or a nice car, the reasoning is very strong and sends signals to the world that you want certain things in your life. However, when you add pictures or images to those thoughts, you inspire them and create a stronger link between what you want and what you brain need as a guide to remember, until it is physically materialized.

It is not enough simply to have an idea or want an event or circumstance to happen. We must give it form as much as possible by using pictures, forms, colors and details. It means that you use the imagination to construct pictures of them, or to "pretend" that in this present time and space you see them. There is always plenty of trust in the operation.

To show what you want is an active artistic interaction between your brain and your ideas and visuals. There is also a part of surrender and trust that it will materialize in the physical form. The first part of the process includes constructive imagination and purpose, the second part refers to our goal and surrender.

This visualization and active creation process stimulate ways of thought and energy that we pass to the world as a possible manifestation. This goes beyond critical thought or pure reflection. We train our minds for these ideas and feelings, and the next step is to expect this to happen. What visuals and pictures do is to allow us to create these thoughts and ideas more vividly?

How to view?

First build a list of things you want to do, feel good, emotions will be a guide and if you feel nice, happy, excited, these are good guides. These emotions are good. If you have questions about anything on your list, it is easier to delete it until your unconscious mind aligns with your thinking.

• Make a list of items you want to say.

• Keep the list reasonable for now, add more things later

• Use optimistic words and make the list as descriptive as possible without a pause

• If an object is, imagine the object with it

• If a scenario is, imagine yourself witnessing the desired circumstance.

• If it's a human, imagine being or talking to him.

You can only spend a few minutes visualizing this list or try to add as many specifics as possible as you want. It is especially productive to imagine early in the morning or before bed. Choose the best time. Try to keep the simulation time consistent so that it becomes part of your lifestyle. With your list and visuals, please have fun. You can buy a newsletter board, a white board or a notebook to help you envision what you want.

Visualization would be like a daydreaming experience. Yet you know it isn't just daydreaming, yet acknowledging life as it is here and now. You trick the mind into thinking that it happens. Sending the success energy to the world magnifies the thought. Your purpose is also a good guide, use your inner guidance to ensure that your visuals are practical to accurate.

Repeat this cycle several times, it could be 10 minutes or a half hour a day, it will be up to you, more time does not make the process work faster.

See how you earn it and fulfill it. Keep working with this process until the target is achieved.

Repeat it, if possible, each day, or work on your vision board by inserting images, expression, or just sitting before your board with the mental goal that you can. You should have no questions when you imagine it. Doubts or convictions which are self-sabotage are stopped so that such feelings do not invade your conscious mind when they seek to disrupt your ideas. Enable them to come and go like a wind, without thinking about it.

Continue with this cycle for as long as it is fun and interesting. When you change them, we change our design also so that our visualization board can undergo any changes over a week or a month. If a goal or desire has changed, make sure that you establish another set of specific priorities or circumstances. Hold it versatile and new. Be versatile, don't think your concepts or vision board should be graved in stone, and make any adjustments if necessary.

If you get the first visual elements, go to the next set of visuals. Remember to spat every time something materialized reveals itself because you put too much energy into it, don't believe it happened either by chance or accident. By the emotional effort you did it. As you see, this fundamental process of manifestation is very basic. Enjoy the trip and have fun.

Guided Visualization & Subconscious Mind Power

Have you ever questioned if something happened or whether you just imagined it happened? If there's a wonderful thing you should learn about the power of your subconscious mind, it is this: it can't say the difference between a true and vibrant experience. It is the theory behind which visualization makes you such an extremely effective tool in your process of becoming your ideal self-image. Once your subconscious embraces new values and behaviors, these shifts are incorporated in your lives. Similar ideas are used in several of my hundreds of audio programs.

The visual influence was seen in a well-known analysis at the University of Chicago a number of years ago. A number of students, all with the same basketball skills, were split into three groups and asked to fire foul shorts. The percentage of baskets created by each team was registered. So, some odd orders were given to the students: the first group was told not to practice or play basketball for 30 days. The second group was told to fire foul shots for 30 days per day for an hour. And the third party was instructed not to go to basketball courts for 30 days at all, but to fire foul shots every day for an hour. The skills of the students were tested at the end of the 30 days. Not surprisingly, Group One, the unpracticed party, performed no better than its original ranking. Group two, the actively practiced party, increased its efficiency by 24 percent. Yet in group three the most impressive findings were found. This group, which didn't foot a basketball court, who just thought about shooting basketball, had increased their performance by 23 per cent, which was almost the same as that of the group which practiced every day.

THE VISUALIZATION POWER

Some of the first athletes to understand watching that could boost performance. A former world class weight lifter hasn't been training seriously for over eight years. He was able to bench 365 pounds when at his best. Nonetheless, during routine exercises, he could never lift more than 280 pounds in recent years. He estimated that 9 to 12 months of rigorous training would be required to get back to the level that he had once achieved and could lift 365 pounds again. This American athlete met the Soviet trainers one evening to show him how to use mental imaging techniques which included very detailed and precise visualizations. The athlete was shocked to find after his mental training that he could comfortably hit a weight he did not lift in eight years, or 365 pounds. An hour of mental preparation makes him do what else at least nine months of rigorous physical exercise would have given him! In recent years, the use of visualization has become very common among professional and Olympic athletes. Studies have shown that visualization can lead to real nerve and muscle changes. Through mixing mental conditioning with real physical activity, these elite athletes are still looking for the edge. Mental changes not only affect physical changes but also the deepest patterns and values. You affect your ideas and values about your self-image and life by visualizing the things you want to achieve. Expanding the pictures of what is possible will resolve what once seemed impossible. The edge of the elite athlete is also your visualization force. Why IT WORKS Visualizations are visual pictures, emotions and ideas about a single event. It's a different phase than simply "seeing" it. Seeing is a physical activity, connected directly with your awake, physical environment. At the other hand, imagining or mental imagery is close to imagination. Your deep-seated convictions about yourself have produced your own portrait. Now, as you are directed through your sessions of relaxation and visualization, you actively use your natural imagination to construct what you really want, beginning with your own image. Every achievement and every piece of art and every worthwhile creation begins as an picture inside a person's mind. Albert Einstein once said, "Imagination is greater than intelligence."

VISUALIZATION: The MENTAL BLUEPRINT FOR SUCCESS

An architect must first of all see the form of building needed in order to construct the house. The vision is then projected onto a sheet of paper: a blueprint. The builders carry out any ideas written on the plan. Visualization functions in the same manner. Throughout your life, the mental picture that you keep in your subconscious mind becomes reality.

HOW TO INCREASE SIMULATION EFFECTIVENESS

The simulation of your day routine can be effective at all times but it is most successful in a relaxed state. Relaxation makes it possible for your visual thoughts to enter your subconscious mind. First, you are relaxed with closed eyes and then release any negative beliefs or feelings about your subject. Instead, with optimistic thoughts and affirmations, you reschedule your mind with strong constructive beliefs and good images.

Various minds function differently, so don't worry if you don't really "see" a mental example or image. Visualizations are often very subtle. You can not see in depth if you are a philosophical thinker. You may obtain thoughts, ideas, feelings or interior knowledge instead, or hear your "inside" ear by perceiving details. You can close your eyes and create vibrant mentally "films"-informative objects, colors, and photographs if you are a visual thinker. And you can obtain both pictures and observations mixed. It is best to escape assumptions of how your views will look. Corrected assumptions or questions about "doing things right" continue to block perceptions. Relax. Relax. Be completely open and sensitive to everything that comes to your inner mind. Your own impressions would be fantastic.

You can encounter a variety of thoughts and images during your visualization sessions that obviously have little to do with your new self image. Such thoughts and photos can, however, be linked to other areas of your life that are somehow related to your self-image. When exposed, they will create those feelings, so you may want to capture these images on your journey to express the sensations. You could find yourself fighting for some of the optimistic images when you start to see a new action or quality — for example, "I could never be that comfortable," or "Forget it; it's just not me." If it's, it's just your mind that answers to a long-time ego's "programming" subconscious. When you start visualizing this pattern reduces and is replaced by the constructive thoughts you now bring into your mind. The positive changes in your life will evolve when you repeat your sessions every day.

It is the analysis which results in applying the law of attraction. The more straightforward you are and the more you understand it, the better it will be, and it will be automatically implemented. The implementation of the rule of attraction is basically just like the overcoming of phobia. It can often feel daunting to face the reality depending on your situation. Yet this feeling is to be overcome and replaced with sheer joy and trust. It takes effort and dedication, as well as persistence and integrity to enforce this rule of attraction. You have to be able to face all your flaws and shortcomings and forgive past problems and resentments. Finally, you must adjust the way you use your feelings to follow the attraction rule. We do this in our thought and while at first it can seem complicated; in practice you can see just how simple and effective this divine change in your consciousness is. To understand how the law of attraction is being applied, think of riding a mountain bike on a ramp off the edge of the cliff with a parachute on your back. That is either an unfortunate thought or it is an exciting thought. That is the feeling connected to the mind. Why is anyone going to do it? The reason is that they are overcome by the feeling of rejoicing. The simple change in what they concentrate on defines the feelings that they experience influenced by the case. Before the individual ever goes on the motorcycle, he "felt" the hustle and bustle of excitation as a wave of consciousness and first through thought and feeling. This helps them to do what other people don't want by enforcing the attraction rule.

It is also best to see for yourself how easily your mood moves in and out of each other as you begin to apply the rule of attraction to your life. Some people want to build a "mood chart," which only tracks what their mood is at present on a pocket notepad. They record it with what they feel is causing a mood shift every time they experience a change of mind. This simple technique shows the influence of moods and "feelings" in their lives for beginners. In only a few days, the influence and the carelessness of the most people, who and what they 'allow to' change the way they feel, will become apparent. You can fully resonate with this definition if you have ever had a bad day. For most people, one unwelcome incident will "ruin" a wonderful day. This can be as simple and trivial as someone leaving the toilet seat or parking. Bam! Bam. Bam! The emotions just like that transform to frustration and the good attitude turns into a bad mood. It can only lead to more things in your day that "harmonize" with your mood, because of the law of attraction.

To apply the rule of attraction is to understand that all of our emotions are messages to the universe. The universe's only job is to respond by transmitting what it receives. So, if you're mad, more stuff will certainly keep you mad, because this is the signal you sent! This applies to all possible emotions, including money, health, relationships, you name them, which deal with all aspects of human concern.

Place a mood log for a couple of days. Scroll back at the performance at the end of the week to watch the best and worst moods. Ask another piece of paper what mood you want to feel all the time around. Go into your log and distinguish positive moods from bad moods. Identify what your mood has shifted between good and bad. Now spend some time in your mind recreating the events. Go back mentally and, after the bad case, find the way to maintain your positive mood. This is one of the secrets of the attraction rules. Know how to protect your good emotions from what the outside world is throwing at you. You have completely learned that if you have mastered the process, you are not a victim of the world. That at any moment of your day you have the ability and power to choose who and how you look, what you attract!

This regulates how you feel to enforce the rule of attractiveness. When a child cries because she does not want to make attempts to do anything with her capacity, people use her feelings to get the attention of a 'higher power' or other people to do something they don't want to. This is a profoundly valid connection, and we were all at some point in our lives guilty of this "emotional disposition." The law of attraction is then developed and established as an emotional entity. Understands how important our thoughts and emotions are, no matter whether we feel drawn to them. They can be knowingly used as artistic instruments or as weapons of destruction unconsciously. Therefore, it is your job to use this power and to learn how to feel good regardless of what it takes.

A second brilliant approach is only to be thankful for the implementation of the law of attraction. Some people are so used to feeling bad that it can be hard to feel good. In this case the law of attraction begins by feeling thankful for any positive thing in your life. This can be just as low as breathing. What's important is to FEEL the consistency of the breathing. Learn how to SENT the emotions of thanksgiving and how to feel happy.

Create a note of what you enjoy. Please invest time to get the top 10 things you're thankful for, which offer you the best sense of love. Type the most frequently used mirror in this list. Whenever you use the mirror, it goes from the top to the bottom mentally through this set. Take your time to use the energy to FEEL the thankfulness and how grateful you are to be. This will take no more than 5-10 minutes, and the implementation of the law of attraction is an extremely effective technique. This works as it creates the habit of seeing the negative through to what you care about!

By focusing your focus on what you care most about and the emotions of affection and gratitude, you draw more of what you want. You better focus your time on what you want and what you don't want! It is always easier. Seek to take a "attitude of appreciation" for yourself. Soon you will know how mighty these two magical words, thank you, are!

The procedures used to enforce the law are as varied as the individuals that use it. You will come up with your own specific methods that work for yourself with some thinking. The end result is that the use of the rule of attraction is to know the ways to feel good in your life and to protect your wallet or bag. You can use your thoughts to enforce the rule of attraction by being mindful of your moods and feelings. We monitor our thoughts directly. We still have power, even though anything bad happens to us.

The application of the law of attractiveness includes efforts not to respond with a negative feeling to something negative. Yet this is what the attraction rule does and takes care of our emotions. You are an old man, so it is not easy to learn how to become an emotional person. It's quick, but research is required. But it is simpler and gradually gets used to it.

When application of the rule of attraction is routine, life is truly flourishing for you! If you have the confidence to face the day, knowing that nothing makes you feel terrible, and you just won't let it happen either. Only because you have chosen to think about what you enjoy, and retain that feeling throughout the day, when you feel fine. If you want to release past hatreds and envy and you know the negative emotions, they are only going to come back to you as negative circumstances. This is fun when the rule of attraction is applied! That's fun when applying the rule of appeal! Which really starts to work and manifest in your life when applying the law of attraction!

Defining Thoughts

You must be prepared to modify the way you use your mind before you can demonstrate the law of attraction. Put aside what you think you know about the world, how it works and the essence of life. Take a step beyond the boundaries of your childhood and creativity program. Suppose that for a moment you are about to discover a secret so profoundly and extremely important that it will change who you are forever. And it will definitely and MUCH quicker than you would ever have anticipated!

The rule of attraction is exactly like that. When you have discussed the law of attraction, it is necessary to bear in mind that it is the fundamental law that regulates all the universe's force. You receive and receive what you give, and you can give it. This is the way and the truth of the world. By having the thoughts and feelings associated with the completed production, you can not create something. Thoughts are born in your head. Ideas produce feelings leading to more ideas, etc. Positive attracts both positive and negative.

The human race is not stopping maturing, but GROWS. The bodies can become their adult forms, but the brains do need to mature in order to understand our full potential. Our key challenge is to control our thoughts and feelings. However, many of us prefer denial of the job, just like an old child who clings to their childhood faith and value system. This takes commitment, discipline, determination, confidence, and these "growing pains," which seem to be doing the same thing, are easy to set aside. The rule of attraction as an intrinsic force is wrong. Everything begins and finishes from inside your mind and nothing can exist without it.

This is not enough to have the rule of attraction clarified. It takes some sincerity, perseverance, bravery and understanding to adjust to this knowledge before our eyes. We live in a world in which we can't make it easier to pick out. We must all know the law of attraction, but above all in our beliefs and reasoning. We must all mature. As a species, our innovations and conditions worldwide place ample pressure on us to evolve psychologically or to face the consequences. We all need to understand and embrace the power available to us in depth and magnitude. Not just to change our own lives, but to turn the world in our wilderness, as we see fit and beyond.

We have fantastic computers in our minds. Far more powerful and complex on this planet than any mechanical tool. It can be used to create and witness something absolute miracles. The brain uses a device that is called the subconscious mind. We users mainly use a conscious gui to use this device. All our unconscious physical actions are regulated by the sub-conscious mind. We are doing 100 thousand other highly critical things from pacing our heart rhythm to releasing enzymes into our bloodstream. The sub-conscious often has a different function, an expression.

All can be broken into smaller parts in the universe. You get to energy when you split it down far enough. So, it's all about electricity! We live and breathe in and are surrounded by bodies made of pure carbon. This is our world and all of this is related, the vibration, pitch, synchronization, harmonization. Essentially, the universe is a vast body of vibration and energy. Now the most important thing is for every human brain to have access to the universe's combined stored power! The subconscious is our link with the infinite force of this energy, pulling any images into our minds.

Our subconscious 'mental duty is simply to build and follow what the user(s) says. And this is the way the emotions are perceived as orders. The subconscious does not discern truth from faith and reacts to every order you offer! You're going to fail if you believe you. You don't, if you think you don't have enough money. These limiting values are what the sub-conscious is ordered to draw from the world. It does what you want every time! Once we reach adulthood, the problem is that we don't use the right commands to draw what we most desire. Sometimes, anxiety, doubt and worry trigger the exact opposite. The newly-found "responsibilities" of young adults produce bad mental patterns of deceit, disappointment or anger.

Turn your life back and find a moment when you are using your subconscious correctly automatically. You were happy, safe, strong and invincible during this time. The planet was your oyster, and you couldn't fulfill any dream in your head. Others never lose this attitude; many never recall thinking like that. In any case, in this joyful mind ALL achievement and happiness are born. We are prepared to use spirits badly. We all seem to have a common shell of suffering and repression through tension and environment. The veil is thick and makes the troubled mind even more burdensome. It's difficult for all of us to leave this mental prison. Yet hope still remains! You can change your life as long as you can remember. After all, it is our thinking that determines us. Too many of us seem to have forgotten that's a great fact. We also find scarves that were collected over the years in our quest to understand the law of attraction. Don't dwell on the suffering that caused them; rather, reflect on how wonderful they feel now and how fantastic their future is in terms of appreciation. Find your life's secret blessings and become your worthy blessed human!

It is not necessary to demonstrate to you plainly the law of attraction. You need to be able to change the way you feel BEFORE you receive anything you want to change your feelings! You have to try to understand your feelings. Thoughts are mixed to generate feelings. Similar emotions are used to form moods. By paying attention to our moods, we can control what we make. You can't analyze your thoughts and track them all, however you can know the mood in which you are. Then just find some way to "ordinary" or improve your moods by shifting your thoughts! Simple and clear right? It's not as easy as it sounds, but it's simpler with practice like anything. We can influence and regulate what we feel through the use of visual images, emotions and imaginations. And the imaginative force of our feelings deliberately aligns with the limitless strength of the universe. To show what we WANT, and to guide our destiny.

These are the 16 best things I've learned successful people don't.

They do not:

1. They do not. Do spend time sorry for yourself. Have the questions I asked brought you into the mind of feeling sorry for yourself is important to you? Okay, remember, productive people are number one and do not murmured and whine. You are not part of such activities, because you take immediate responsibility and you talk and whine about your decisions and get your mind to think about itself and its intent. You're not involved. Returns are part of a good report, and also gives a good individual an appreciation of his conduct and actions that of an individual whose mind is well balanced. If a good person experiences a reversal, the difference is that they're going to say, "Okay, it happened, next." You realize that housing digs for you just a deeper pit, and no one profits.

2. Cringe of change. Cringe of change. A good person knows that transition is part of life. Change happens and the only thing people are concerned about is how the transition is handled. A good person requires an instantaneous stance and mindset to consider change and

see it as a opportunity. They begin to see change as new and exciting opportunities to evolve, better their lives, gain knowledge, and because of this optimistic mindset a shift can become the best setting for productive work.

3. Make their strength. Make their strength. A good individual knows that his power is far stronger than he actually does. A power lies in the way they respond. I had a brand-new car that smelled inside it and the car wouldn't start on a morning after a few months that I was not necessarily late, but I would be late if I didn't stay on the stage. It's been accounted for every minute. Okay, it wouldn't be that morning when I started my car. A couple of times, I remember trying and yet no control. I called Triple "A" and they told me it'd take over an hour to get to me. Perhaps there's something God is salvaging me from, so I changed, I thought to myself after the call to Triple "a." I haven't been mad, mad or sad. Because of my lack of emotion, I had the ability to stay in the right mindset and I could think outside of the box and hold the conference over the phone, saving the money, time and energy going to the meeting over the phone. All worked out, thus. Know that successful people keep their feelings and actions under control and don't give someone else or anyone else control.

4. Tackle things that are out of your control, time or money. A good person can't waste a minute outside his influence on issues. You realize that they can not manage

anything, long queues, other irritating circumstances. It is just the time waste the wastes precious time on items which are not important and inefficient. Good people understand completely that such things can not be regulated, as well as that it is unproductive to waste expensive time and energy worrying.

5. Risk of terror. The four-letter word is one that brings fear in most people and is "danger." Danger is not something people fear because they are danger-takers by their very nature. If I put it this way, I have to assume that most people are going to change their viewpoint and attitude about risks. Let us use the word opportunity instead of using the word danger. The reason I want you to change this word danger is that many people believe that it's a tentative situation to leap into. Successful people handle circumstances carefully, creatively and actively.

6. Concern what other people think. That attribute is known as finesse and is used by successful people in their DNA. As we all want people to like us, successful people know that it's not possible. You don't understand what you do, because that can be like solving poverty in the world, someone doesn't like it, it's going to happen. They realize that they can not and won't be fulfilled by anyone, so that they handle situations and circumstances with compassion, integrity and justice.

7. Two times make the same mistake. Many times, people will spend a great deal of time pontificating an unpleasant event, decision or circumstance. That's exactly what effective people don't do. Every loss is an opportunity to learn. They're first to try not to do it again. They don't waste time in the land of crazy, they do the same thing time and again. Those who excel become better acquainted.

8. Live for fame. Live for fame. What would make a difference in the past? NEVER! It is understood by productive men. Nobody benefits from lingering and worrying about the past, particularly if it is a negative thing. Successful people invest and the growth of their minds is focused on building a wonderful present that they realize is the only thing they can improve and prepare for a better future!

9. Just give up. Give up. Still! Still! Give up what? Give up what? That's what a good person always says to himself. Renunciation is not a choice that a good person can not recognize if they are giving up. The only choice they have is perseverance and the target.

10. Envy others. Envy other men. Productive people find motivators for other effective people. You use the performance of these people to inspire and not to criticize. Successful people have the overall attitude of joy for the

success of others, because they realize that the stage is wide and everyone has space. You do know you deserve to be there because you're on the stage.

11. Save the hour for yourself. They just enjoy spending some time dreaming and planning alone. While a good person is content with others, he / she may be able to rest or sit alone.

12. Look forward to quick progress. In the long term, productive people are in it. You love this cycle and expect the victory. You realize that it takes time to prepare and execute this program. Patience is your friend and you know what a virtue it really is. There are no inadequate or unrealistic aspirations for successful people. You recognize that their progress may take a long time; therefore, it is not wise to expect immediate results.

13. Three. Feel something is owed. Perhaps the most troublesome working people on earth are wealthy people. Such people grow mobile phones, which we love, launch a breast cancer initiative and make pink amazing, do what they want to do, but we enjoy watching them at games, or on TV, or setting up a system to speak to our family and friends. Good people are not reliant on their qualifications or past accomplishments. You know like you have no right to have the world at your feet. We are not motivated to

work for whether they want a big salary, a great title, amazing benefits or a free lunch.

14. Currently, value capital. Successful people know that time is their most precious thing. You know you can lose $100,000 a day or you can make $100,000 a day, but you can't get back that day. So, you arrange what you do and use your energy.

15. They write things down, based on memory. The Bible tells me to write and explain the dream. It is better for a good person than anyone. You know, if you don't type it, you probably don't remember the specifics. You know. They also recognize that by writing it down, a clear action plan can be followed. Since successful people are planners who write down things, it defines their priorities, and they are more likely to put their hopes and aspirations before them as an accountability device. Successful people are humble enough to know that nobody in their minds alone can remember a plan.

16. Talk more than you hear and watch. Successful people understand how consummate students can be. They must always be students to perfect their company. Successful people acknowledge the need for a higher degree of expertise and understanding than average. I've just watched a documentary by Michael Jackson and he said he always asked questions. He wished to be a perfect man.

While perfection is elusive to all of us, one thing I know is that we can come closer if we strive for it.

CHAPTER NINE: MOTIVATE YOURSELF

You won't do something with four dreaded letter words-job in several days. There will be no time. Whatever kind of work you do with a particular purpose, often we need the explosion of energy to battle the 'lazy,' 'procrastinating,' 'I-want-to - do' voice in our heads.

It is that, but it is important to understand how you get into equipment quickly so you can take action. Everybody goes through it. Motivating yourself is one of the best ways. Here are 10 strategies that are successful anytime you think encouragement is important.

Seeing the future gives you inspiration to realize what you want in life. A vision of your perfect life should be provided. Where would you like to travel? Where would you live? Where would you like to live? In one of the world's stunning beaches you could be sailing on Yacht. You could live in a house with a lovely wife and children playing around. Since a teenager you might purchase this dream car you have always wanted. Put a collage on the wall and location. Be not afraid to let others see it because it motivates you to do your work. It's not for someone else, it's for you.

Go out and run Yes, run. Probably, for you, it's really safe. You'll be running to stimulate your brain with blood and help you to think better and get more oxygen in your body. However, the idea is to get you away from all the hustle and bustle of your mind and just enjoy all that's happening outside. Perhaps you can just jog around and watch people water the lawn, children play outside, people chat and support each other, etc. Life is far more than stuck at work, so it is often a easy but effective incentive to get your phenalene flowing when you see something else besides your job.

Everyone has role models to get inspiration from Gurus. There are a lot of people who are fascinated by features in wildest circumstances. Donald's a perfect example. I mean Donald Trump. He had more than $900 million in debt, but he managed to get out to become one of the richest men on earth, after 10 years of experience. Some research may be required to analyze your biography, but it is useful. Look for inspiration and learn about who is working in the same area on which you work. Post an image of them on your wall and use their journey to success to inspire you whenever you feel.

Only take action Believe it or not, it is crazy for others to feel inspired to get to work. If you act, you will find the inspiration comes to you if you are closely associated with your job. You're going to witness the momentum! An example might make you hate something and then immerse yourself in it and make it into an obsession. As you act, you may gradually be more conscious of and improve all the little stuff you've previously not noticed, which may intrigue you, inspire you to dive deeper into your work.

Many people can not be inspired if they don't feel pain or pressure to do something. Stimulating pain There are periods of desperation where there is no choice but to work. This kind of "urgency" gives a person an energy burst to do things. You can make pain by returning and recalling the traumatic repercussions that you had to do something, even if you don't do something like screaming from someone you are scared of or the feeling of living on the streets without a home. You can build pain.

It was one of the scariest men on this earth; I remember my fresh high school baseball coach; we'd listen every time he was barking. I figured it would be an enjoyable basketball experience, but it inspired each one of us to compete, sacrifice and battle for our lives, or we would be even more penalties and eventually be cut off from our family. This was a physically live nightmare. Often discomfort is the greatest incentive because we don't have control and don't want to speak out about our acts because we feel relaxed with ourselves.

Are you the best blood thirsty? Rivalry Will you have the killer instinct to deal with your adversaries? Where more than one person wants to do the same in any field of work, rivalry will always take place no matter what. Some people hate it, some use it to make them happier and work harder. You may be aware of the people you see and do not see right now and place them on your board, because you know it is the target to beat, to get ahead, to win. Move to the "top of the fittest" mode and use this push to make you compete while you're thinking.

Music The music has an influence on our mood, not a brainer. You're going to feel sad when you put on a blues tune. You're going to be comfortable if you put on a jazz tune. You're going to be happy if you put on pop music. You will feel inspired if you put on a motivational tune. And how many songs you will consider like this? Millions and millions and people. People have various music habits that influence them, just find a music that motivates them. Songs that inspired me typically have a fast rhythm. When you like hip-hop, consider listening to Tupac or Eminem's "Changes."

Laughter production Laughs your inspiration. Life does not always have to be difficult, nor does it always need an amazing, beautifully planned form of motivation. Often you just have to laugh well, throw aside your fears and go on. Imagine a funny thing in the past that made you laugh so stupidly, or if your goodness changes, take a present scenario and make it so unbelievably meaningless that it makes you laugh too. You can use your own self-representation, be dumb, be a fool for a while, imagine that the job is amusing. It is a great feeling, using irony. Using humor.

Small bits One little, small, single, small ... Small bits Step goes a long way. Phase goes a long way. If you feel like you can't get to work, do just one thing, even though it is the least likely thing. Every time you take a small move, then award yourself. Check on the back of yourself. It is supposed to be a psychological influence to make you believe that you do more work than you do, but the end results do that you do work, so why not go ahead with it.

I hated mathematics homework at high school, for example. I'd be moving it onto the side several times. I noticed that if I just took the strength to open my wallet, flip it onto my homework page and just watch it for a few seconds, I knew I could do the first three problems at least. Then I could do the next one and the next. I'd subconsciously be doing my homework before I knew it.

Finally, you know why you work? Do you know why you work? Or are you working blindly for no reason? We do it for a reason and sometimes it will be enough to inspire you if you know exactly why you are doing what you do. Perhaps that is beyond materialism, whether it is to assist a lover or to get out of a horrible circumstance, or perhaps it is more to do with personal growth. How do you want to do that? Whatever it is, make sure that what you want is what motivates you to do and why when you think about it. You are helped in doing so.

What is the driving thing for me?

There is not one thing that motivates me in particular. Typically, during this particular period, I am inspired by random events that occur around me. Nonetheless, what really helps to inspire me is to know what happens if I do it. What the result or result of something is all about. What would be inevitable.

For example, I know that I can learn new things, if I take the time to read a book. It isn't always a pleasure to read sometimes, but I know that at least I can get something out of it, so it's enough to inspire me to act. And if you do anything enough, you know, not only for the short term but for the long term, what would result? Look forward. Look forward. Look forward. I mean, motivation is often important for that short burst of energy to give you, but in the end, you would prefer to use it to create an inevitable outcome because you know it will happen before you. Do not depend every single time on motivation to do something.

Steps to Self Motivation

1. Performance Plan A successful project requires time and careful preparation as a first step. You intend to fail if you fail to prepare. Timing for the correct preparation can be challenging, but this time it is important to get a risk off the ground. You could wake up fifteen minutes early and go to bed fifteen minutes later, but this time you will never regret it because it's well spent.

The first order is to decide what you want to do. This will include a list of goals relevant to your topic. Placing gold is an intrinsic craft. The target will be a long-term objective in two phases – firstly, and then each aim as smaller objectives or tasks in bite-size pieced pieces. Then placed these targets into a plan or a goal map.

You will find the steps needed to achieve the long-term target once you have your target chart. Now set a date for every small target when you expect each job to be done. Once each mission is completed to accomplish a long-term goal, make sure you circle this on your target map so you can keep track of your progress.

Now you meet to list your "how" goals, which makes your feelings that much stronger and easier in mind. You just ought to get to the root cause of why you want to accomplish these goals. Perhaps you want your children to have more time or send them to a good school. Perhaps you want to fly around and see the world. Make sure you define these "why s" when you can.

2. Delete negative actions There will still be people who seem in one way or another against you and your performance. All these people can't be excluded because some of them will be your kin. The trick is that you know your excitement doesn't understand exactly why you want improvement in life.

However, you can do some things to minimize negativity. The first thing you can do is eliminate as many ads as you can. Five years ago, without television, television or news magazines in my life, I went to the media easily. I started with the idea to try 30 days, but I found that I have just felt so good since then. The news media is full of negativity. You need to remove the power of the media if you want to lead a healthy life.

3. Another way of eliminating negativity is to enjoy a diet free of toxins, sugar and processed food. Consuming a

healthy diet with the absence of these dangerous and toxic chemicals your mental stability and intent will be enhanced. Keep food in its normal state. Special attention is paid to fresh fruits and vegetables and lean protein sources. Minimize grain and milk intake. Every day make sure that a safe source consumes plenty of water.

4. When you eliminate uncertainty from life, it helps to clear your mind. De-Clutter Your Life. When you prepare, ensure that your time in the office stays smooth. As you prepare. You do not have the ability to focus your mind on artistic issues if you stay at work or are entangled. You will focus on the need to clean the place, because your subconscious mind knows that it must be clean to flow your creativity.

If the routine is going every week, it removes the burden of getting behind in seeing piles of paper and clutter. This therefore makes your planning phase a priority.

5. Physical exercise strengthens mind and body. Nutrition Blood supply, energy and mental control are enhanced. It doesn't mean that you have to work out every day for three hours to get better. Just 30 minutes a day of strict physical activity will improve dramatically over time.

So, make sure you add 30 minutes a day for the physical activity while you're preparing your goals. Choose and adapt every day the things that you enjoy. This means that the training program doesn't get bored and leaves.

6. "If the eyes are the window of the soul, posture is the window of wellbeing." Many physiological changes occur in the body while you are maintaining a healthy posture. The first thing that changes is that the respiration is done better as the lungs develop fully. Good posture also helps the spinal cord to remain calm, preventing pinching nerves or subluxations.

This helps to alleviate the pain that distracts you from any effort. It increases food flow into the brain and increases the mind concentration and focusing capacity. Another great benefit is good posture.

7. Sleep The time you spend sleeping is very critical if you want to achieve your objectives. Sleep is when the body becomes younger and the mind is most imaginative. So I advise that you sleep for seven to eight hours a day so that you don't want to be sleepless.

I always recommend keeping a dream diary next to your bed so you can catch the imaginative thoughts your mind produces whenever you wake from a dream.

8. Meditation is an ancient type of prayer, in fact. When you meditate your brain produces frequencies to calm, reflect and rejuvenate. This means clearing the mind in order to connect with God better. Meditation clears the mind of emotions that divert your attention from your goals.

One of my favorite meditation techniques I give my patients is the exercise I ask for. You imagine yourself sitting around on a warm summer day during this exercise. You plunge into all the sound, smell, and beauty of the essence of the waters. Then you turn to a single location in the center of the lagoon where only the water can be seen. Your only job is to keep the water still and cool.

Each thinking you think is a pebble that hits and rips the mud. When those waves happen, the water needs to be cooled again so that the water surface is like glass. In the first case, you can keep this state only for seconds at a time, but in practice, you can actually reach a point at which you can free your mind from disturbance of thought.

9. Affirmations It is an affirmation that uses a short, optimistic and repeated thinking to help concentrate your mind on what you want in your life. Affirmations are an

incredibly helpful method in drawing in your life what you want. Make sure the outlook is constructive, reliable and current. Please write down your comments and show them to you.

Repeat your comments to yourself and where possible aloud during the day. At least they should be repeated multiple times before they wake up and fall asleep.

10. Motivational quotes Motivational quotes are a perfect way to inspire you quickly! Every one has a gift to change life for better, inspired by its story.

Many of them come from well-known people and some from unknown writers, but every time they get a few words they need to learn and develop. In places where I see them every day, I like to hold motivational quotes.

Motivational quotes have also spun incredible achievements throughout history and have given many people tremendous inspiration in past times. You can find motivational quotes, write them down, hold them with you, and allow this inspiration to sink down into your subconscious mind.

11. Visualization To visualize means to see it in the palm of your mind. It will inspire you to take action and make this thinking a reality with enough strength and emotion. Therefore, if we see an outcome in our minds, it must be seen as real.

Consider every aspect of the outcome you like. Do you want to visit this place? So, imagine it all; the way it looks, the way it sounds, the people and animals that will surround you. Make it all so clear in your mind about this place.

Then all the feelings you'd like to be in this place begin to experience. When it comes to visualization, emotions are strength. It's the gas that takes you where you want to go. You know it. You may also want to create a vision board or images related to things that you desire in life, so that you can look at them in inspiration every day.

If it's a place that you want to visit, or a house that you want, or what you want in life, imagination helps you get there ... Great luck! Good luck!

12. Do you know when to go on holiday? Do you recall a to - do list? Do you know the day before you are about to go on holiday? On that day, most people keep a to - do list to

make all the important things happen before they leave the house.

Should not be as successful every day as the day before you leave for holiday? You can build the day by your choice every morning. Whether there are goals to do, or things to do to evolve, you can make a blueprint for your day by writing it down. It makes you more efficient and gives you a sense of fulfilment when your list is reviewed for every item.

13. Three. Telephone a Friend The best thing to put you out is the link to an old friend. It is a strong thing to witness all the best moments, even though it's over the internet. Communication and laughing are a perfect way to improve the mood. Touch someone and reach out!

14. Get a makeover Seek a makeover if you just want to be inspired. Just try another hairstyle, purchase new clothing, get a special perfume or cologne, and maybe wear some new jewels. Purchasing new products makes you feel relaxed and secure in your presentation to others.

15. Maintain a newspaper A diary is an ideal way to stay inspired with the passing of time. It took me just 5 minutes a day to write down the challenges and successes during the day. I once had a teacher who told me, "If it is worth it

is worth writing down." You will chronicle where you were and see how far you have really evolved. That is significant.

With a newspaper your day and how you spent time are made accountable. You'll be less likely to do things that don't suit your goals if you know that you have to write will night before bed. The most difficult teacher to please you can consider.

In this way, I like journaling. First of all, I clear up my mind and equate my list with what I have done in the past. I get my past out of the day. I will then write down any challenges or successes that I have faced all day long. Then the next day I'm making my to - do list.

16. Take a holiday Take a holiday to relax and feel rejuvenated. It is like using an over and over saw without ever having time to sharpen it and going too longer without a break. Take your time, then, and sharpen the sight.

17. Have a waiting mentality!

You should expect changes in all facets of your life if you do only a few of the tasks you regularly discuss in this course. Don't be coy about what your life wants. It is a short life, and if you want to make the most of it, you'll make those things a self-motivated human.

CHAPTER TEN: PLAN YOUR LADDER OF SUCCESS AND GET STARTED

It is the right of man to achieve all grandeur, and success really should be his practice. Man is basically perfect, and therefore the possibilities of him are infinite.

To bring out the best indoors, a life well lived that is structured and disciplined to explore the potentials that lie inside us.

The main point is not how many talents each of us has, but how necessary we should focus on discovering, leveraging, exploring and applying our current skills, qualities and abilities in our daily lives.

The question you have to ask is can you use at least one great talent that resides inside you in practical terms? The only fundamental principle is to recognize that all our progress depends solely on us.

The best way to be glad is to do the stuff you want and want to do naturally – something you truly love! The best way to excel and become rich, too, is to make sure you achieve the things in life you are excited to strive for. It will allow you to make attempts to assess the progress of activities.

For example, a simple way of describing this is to consider: if you are interested in the art, painting and drawing, you have to look for guidance on how to participate in competitions and how to show your artwork through galls or fine art publishers or even reveal your skills through galleries (address galleries directly and leave works on a sale or return basis).

In order to optimize your capacity to attract a large audience with interests in various subjects, you may want to add many types of topics to your art portfolio.

Contacts, blogs and even Internet news channels, explore different ways (such as photographers, image gallery and framing books, arts councils, government agencies that offer funding, including loans, etc.) to improve the enquiry.

With regard to your issue, postal questions, polls, surveys, decides what people want, and then just searches for the need and fills it out.

Every little can help but it's the power to take the momentum and that is the most important thing. Another important point is not only to try and continue to try, but rather build a mindset from which you can obey, adopt and apply the techniques that have been discussed here.

Finally, don't hesitate-keep faith and don't give in to any loss. If you have agreed to execute the 'plan,' make sure it stays lit and loud ... rejects and deceptions do not in any way diminish your optimism, success and desire to succeed. Thousands of people who have succeeded in the last few days, amid all the challenges, pain and hardships, have inspired many millions around the world.

You must bear in mind that various individuals may have specific methods of accumulating wealth, but the aim is similar to everyone and the steps previously listed are successful in your overall success.

To grow internally, very strong will is required, and it is important that we have two main characteristics, namely courage and trust. Poverty and wealth therefore don't inherently depend solely on expertise (e.g. business capacity, marketing techniques, etc.) but definitely depend on the three cs, which are character, imagination and innate capacities.

Courage and faith alone can bring about a profound change, while in times of turmoil and crisis the other hand can bring only great sorrow and despair. However, in spite of the problems of life we should avoid obstacles and barriers and constantly note the ultimate intrinsic or natural force which we are all able to cultivate effectively through spiritual insight.

Without these attributes you will struggle, which is why a vast number of people feel frustrated when they compete or simply give up under strain, due to a lack of self-consciousness and complex force of will.

There is a propensity for us to return to old ways, when our desires and aspirations are not met-the hollowness we feel can be highly disturbing and we can't always ignore it. Most of the time, it does not mean that anything good we do with our life is going to go on. This is not because we need discipline that isn't possible, but because we lack confidence and trust we are overcome by the negative attitude.

The initial excitement starts fading, and what seemed so glorious transforms into a dangerous dilemma and problem. The mind takes over and questions override doubts after doubts about the meaning of the entire idea / concept – a disagreement occurs, the intellect tells the one thing and our intuition encourages us to pursue the road to 'development.'

The end is inevitable even before we begin the journey, because we do not determine which true direction to take. Success lies in what you're not doing (do not fantasies success). What you think it would be.

So how can we begin?

The primary thing to help you discover the objective of success is your mindset and then how you behave. These two characteristics are essential in accordance with a collection of clear principles. Reason-based thoughts are a strong source of action and you soon know that bravery is the basic virtue that a human being requires to cross the rocky path.

Barriers to acquiring money, as I am sure you would accept, are inevitable and are a way to do so. Perseverance, persistence and perseverance must be diligently exercised so that the goal is accomplished and the challenges overcome. Of course, I would like now to illustrate the P's on which you have to frown.

Don't go on, don't think you know it all and don't last your 'venture(s).' Be ready to battle the stumbling blocks, but follow your target and allow your force of will to prevail.

In all life circumstances, with all the ups and downs that we may face, it's obviously necessary to stay focused. Recall that existence is by definition dualistic-the opposite and reverse sides of the same coin. I would add that, while we know that the past is the cause and the present is the consequence, it is clear that the present itself is the trigger for the future.

This syntax has a very deep sense, and if you can link this to achievement, then it can be said that we will become the architects of our own future if we live in scientific self-discipline with intellect.

The following instructions will help you pave the way for your ultimate success.

The measures in your daily life are really easy to follow.

1. Do what you love and good at. Do what you want.

2. Be eager and prepared to learn (motivation and excitement).

3. To be a creative guy.

4. Be willing to spend your time, energy and resources, and not just money.

I listed money-this does not mean you must spend a great deal in order to become a millionaire or a rich man.

5. You have to be diligent to set goals and objectives. Recall that perseverance is the secret to success.

6. You need to be able to efficiently handle your time.

7. Learn how to give back to society as you grow. Philanthropy, I call it.

You need a strong vision – one in which you "make" yourself succeeding. Good people of the past and the present ensure that by taking these basic steps they achieve this coveted role.

However, in step 2, for a very good reason, I used the word 'know' intentionally. Life is the greatest teacher, and you must always be prepared to question yourself (using the power of discrimination) and thus learn the glorious truth that you learned over time by its eternal principles. This means that when the time comes, you have to act.

Action is extremely necessary and the achievement of the two is synonymous with integrity. Action is important to succeed, but how serious you are is the critical component. Too serious can ruin your business, so FUN is key.

Any discipline is organized and orderly. You must be able to hear your inner voice as much as you can, as I described in the introduction. It means that you start having faith in your strengths instead of being too dependent on your family, friends and so forth (not that it is bad).

Stand alone, aim for progress and learning. Frequently, failures will arise from the cases in which we avoid practicing our own opinions, or become too reliant on others 'opinions.

Success is not a mystery you need to dig for or discover for to your destination. Instead, it's your perception or acceptance of what you really want in life. Intuition, confidence, abilities, awareness, obstacles and prospects are terms that characterize the characteristics of wealthy people. Any job completed in the right way will reward you. Mental attitudes are what will get you prosperity, but negative attitudes, faintheartedness and effort will contribute to failure.

Don't expect too much in a short time, but your attitude should be constructive and perfectly execute your mission and concentrate on your long-term goal(s). And you are focusing on your mission and you are correctly executing your plans. That ought to be your life philosophy.

To order to start a new project, it is important that you understand the following. You must understand that you must be acquainted with the term cash flow in order to start a company. Capital expenditure is a requirement but, above all, the idea of the sustainability of the business is of the utmost importance.

Steps to determine personal wealth can be the most difficult step in your quest to start your journey into wealth. The problem is that before you get into yourself and unlock your inherent qualities you are likely to be reluctant and indecisive. It's not untrue, but it can't motivate you to reach your full potential more often than not.

There is no barrier to your full potential being unleashed-it is your ability to listen to your inner voice that lies 'hidden.' The effort to take advantage of a great opportunity is a methodical approach to the job.

Sit still, sooth your thoughts and senses and meditate on the subject. Only because the idea seems appealing, don't rush into something at once. In the initial step, much appears to be very fine, but thinking, preparation and time are a precondition. It's always something that asks you what to do. The key can not actually be accessed from the outside, but from the inside.

The little secret that will help you amass riches is to aspire to do your best at all times. The ability to visualize (I mean positive imagination) is an essential element in creative thinking-but you can not do so without a strong will, and particularly the faculty of visualization has to be matured into firm belief and conviction.

1. You must want to achieve your popularity target – this is rule number one.

2. Be prepared to deal with schedule, spending, responsibility and/or transparency effectively.

3. Don't spend more than you need and spend less than you do.

4. Financial issues may be ruinous, like drug addiction, etc. It has to be achieved from the very beginning.

5. Find ways to spend and start saving money in particular. You have to play intelligently and get your goals right.

You can face a lot of antagonism in every company, a lot far from an ideal situation. Expectations, hope and the urge to "wish" that things go as expected will lead to disappointment and often.

This makes preparation very important for your success, as discussed earlier. The other considerations that must be taken into account are also work and fatigue, of course. With the expectation of making the millions, you are likely to be a disillusioned mess and disillusioned-not helpful in progressing or finding money.

When you continue to refuse to accept defeat, realize that by complex determination the goal you have set yourself to accomplish materializes.

Thoughts can be extraordinarily powerful instruments. And you can certainly achieve your goal if you are able to follow this divine gift. When you cling to some complex will powered thinking, it takes on a tangible external form.

Then it is time for the negative features of routines, lack of good preparation, lack of confidence, uncertainty and ignorance of life as a whole. You have the power to do whatever you want; the power lies in the heart. Lack of focus is the root cause of life failure-don't take your ideas, principles, and tactics at once in the hope of success. Start your goals slowly and be consistent.

Focus on one thing at a time and let your MIND not go 'over move' state .. Concentrations are a logical way of doing them, and the magic word is relaxation when completing all the activities at the right pace.

Do not rush and cause confusion, but instead concentrate your whole mind methodically and carefully on everything you do and keep your mind flexible.

When you know you really are on the right track and on the road to your target, be vigilant with time management. It is also tempting to invest so much in a project that you can get carried away to perfect everything you do.

You have to prioritize your job and appreciate the importance of time and appreciate it – don't waste your time and life!

The key to success

The environment plays an enormous role as I have said, as it is very unavoidable – especially for us inside.

A calm, confident person is much more probable than his / her equivalent, a winner in a difficult situation, a person who was stressed and irritated. The former has completely associated his senses with his own world.

The anxious person therefore does not understand the situation and thus finds himself in trouble. The keywords in life are concentration, concentration and attention.

1. Develop a simple and definite goal.

2. Create a working plan / program that is wise.

3. Protect your safety. Protect your family. There's no real wealth without fitness.

4. Your energy must be stored.

5. Be truthful (in words, actions, feelings, actions) in your life.

6. Keep to values and follow sound principles.

7. Think of ideal personalities and look to their ideology for energy.

8. Seek the guidance of God and be true.

9. Start of supporting and gratefully serving others.

Nine. Still believe in God's strength and think positive.

The path to success is indeed transformative thinking. Plan your target and consciously ruminate and know the importance of this strategy.

Since time immemorial great people from all walks of life were the true victors, which is why they train their minds to be content. Ethical discipline, particularly self-discipline, is important.

Each person is singular. What is perfect for A may not be appropriate for B. However, it must be pointed out that everybody can appreciate harmony, isolation, silence and integrity. Everyone has experienced harmony at some level or other, regardless of age, caste, religion, color, sex.

You will decide the precise way to design your mind's complex body and thus reach great heights after discovery by means of test and error.

Meditation may not be successful for all, but that doesn't mean you don't improvise these methods if needed.

Be systematic and use methods which bring you success and happiness, your only goal must be.

Our intellectual abilities decide our behavior, and the mind should be domed and controlled quite obviously. Constant diligence is required and the ongoing training of the mind paves the way for ultimate success.

CONCLUSION

Begin to live in a positive mental attitude right now. Be optimistic and confident instead of being pessimistic. Fill your mind with hope and positive expectations instead of concern and uncertainty. Substitute the fear and self-doubt mindset with a burning desire and utter confidence in your success.

Their emotional or behavioral disposition reflects a fundamental difference between rich and poor, the good and the bad, the fortunate and the unfortunate. The way we respond to circumstances and opportunities that come our way defines our mental attitude. In general, the wealthy typically have a rich mental attitude, while the poor typically have an unconscious mental attitude.

Picture two human minds to explain. A rich mentality and a bad mentality. As a glittering, new car zooms by, both standing side by side on the roadside. All smile with awe at the car and watches it vanish around the corner.